"*Kingdom Students* makes the very important point that all students—not just those who are studying to be pastors or missionaries—should see their time in school as preparation for a lifetime of service in God's kingdom. If Jesus's lordship is as wide as creation, it is as wide as culture. And if it is as wide as culture, it is as wide as the whole curriculum at a given school or college. Highly recommended."

—**Bruce Ashford**, provost and dean of faculty,
Southeastern Baptist Theological Seminary

"I love how this book, from the very beginning, emphasizes the need for students to be kingdom focused. Education isn't just about learning or job placement; it's about preparing individuals to serve God and his people. Christianity is no respecter of intellect—the brilliant and the simple are called to the kingdom, and they enter on equal footing. I'm very thankful for this book, and it's my desire and hope to see every student read this and apply it in their lives. Now has to be the time we, youth workers, prepare our students for a life of loving God and serving his people."

—**Jay Barbier**, youth specialist, Tennessee Baptist Mission Board

"God is raising up a generation of college students who are seeking first the kingdom of God and his righteousness as they pursue their education. This book, written by my friends Cory Barnes and Norris Grubbs, is exactly the sort of resource those students need to begin their college journey on the right track. I'm excited to see how the Lord uses this book in the lives of kingdom students."

—**Nathan A. Finn**, provost and dean of the
university faculty, North Greenville University

"Without a doubt, this book will enlighten your mind, strengthen your servanthood, and bring your future into a clearer focus as you seek to glorify God while pursuing your education. With a career spanning over three decades in higher education, I found the definition of my calling in the pages of this book. Well done!"

—**Lynn Gibson**, vice president for enrollment
services, Blue Mountain College

"A big challenge many students face when starting their college career is valuing learning academic and life skills, like note-taking and productivity. Barnes and Grubbs provide a clear and compelling argument for why we should develop these skills that help every student be successful in their studies and thrive wherever God leads them. Their use of 'kingdom students' frames this endeavor along the lines of seeing how your efforts in college will help you fulfill your kingdom calling. They also have done a great job including many practical ways to develop these important skills. As someone who teaches a freshman introductory course, I recommend this book to those who have the privilege of teaching this group of students."

—**Jonathan C. Grenz**, dean, School of Ministry,
Palm Beach Atlantic University

"*Kingdom Students: Skills to Succeed in Education and the Rest of Your Life* would be an extremely beneficial read for anyone; no matter their age, career, or educational status. However, I say unequivocally this is a must-read for every student beginning their college career. Cory Barnes and Norris Grubbs give a clear challenge for students to pursue more than just a degree during their college years, and their life is about far more than just having a job. Barnes and Grubbs enable the reader to see their life from a biblical perspective and that God-given opportunities must be seized today!"

—**W. Thomas Hammond Jr.**, executive director/
CEO, Georgia Baptist Mission Board

"Setting priorities and deciding what you want from your college experience is half the battle in getting the most from your college and post-graduate education. Barnes and Grubbs give solid foundational principles for your education and give a practical, strategic blueprint for mastering the expectations of professors. Moreover, they give solid wisdom on how a God-centered, kingdom mindset will shape every aspect of your life as a student and set essential patterns for the rest of your life. This is a perfect preparation book for students stepping into the world of academia, giving a wonderful blend of practical tips for success in the classroom with foundational principles for aligning priorities and developing a life around Christ's calling."

—**Jerry Johnson**, campus minister, Baptist
Collegiate Ministries, University of Georgia

KINGDOM STUDENTS

KINGDOM STUDENTS

Skills to Succeed in Education and the Rest of Your Life

CORY BARNES
and
NORRIS GRUBBS

B&H
ACADEMIC
NASHVILLE, TENNESSEE

For Our Wives and Children:

Kim, Katie, Mollie, and Cameron Grubbs—my cup runneth over.

Kayla, Zoey, and Noel Barnes—It is not good for the man to be alone.

. . .

Also, we extend appreciation and gratitude to our colleagues at New Orleans Baptist Theological Seminary and Shorter University.

CONTENTS

FOREWORD

College. It's more than just four years of school that enable you to get a better-paying job while also having a lot of fun. A person's college experience marks some of the most influential years in his or her life. Students, it will be during these years that you develop deep friendships that last a lifetime. It will be during these years that most of your ideological views will develop. It will be during these years that most of you will meet your spouses. And it will be during these years that you begin to figure out who you are, what you really like, and how you want to spend the rest of your life. Your college years are important years indeed!

This is especially true for Christians. In addition to all of the above, Christians are called to live as ambassadors for Christ (2 Cor 5:20). That is, we are called to live in a world that is not our own and while here, we are tasked with representing the interests of our King and his kingdom. We are called to spend our lives in such a way that his kingdom is built, his church is made strong, his people are made whole, and his name is honored. As such, as Christians develop ideologically, make lifelong friends, figure out their passions, and potentially meet their future spouses, it is vital that this happens with the kingdom in clear view. These years in college should be spent taking every opportunity to develop for maximal impact for the kingdom. If we are to fulfill the Great Commission, it will take every member of the body of Christ. Yes, it will take the preachers and the missionaries. But it will also take the teachers, the doctors and nurses, the businessmen and -women, the lawyers, the police officers, the builders, and more. It will take the whole body of Christ working together, infiltrating the fabric of society, and there in those places where we work and live, leveraging our lives for the cause of Jesus Christ. For the Christian, therefore, the college years are especially important!

But what kind of development must take place for us during these years, and how do we navigate these years most successfully? There are a lot of areas that could be mentioned in response to such a question, but four particular areas of development are especially important. In this volume, Cory Barnes and Norris Grubbs, two highly effective Christian educators, help Christian students think through their approach to academics, productivity, leadership, and relationships. They show us why our academic pursuits are important, why we need to maximize these years with optimal productivity, why we need to develop as leaders, and why we need to approach our relationships wisely. And for each of these matters, they help us to see how to do all it with the kingdom in mind at every step.

This is exactly the kind of book that I, as the president of New Orleans Baptist Theological Seminary and Leavell College, want my students to read and reflect on. May we all approach our preparation and work with a sense of purpose and the kingdom in mind. I trust that this book will prove helpful for you in that journey.

—James K. Dew Jr.

INTRODUCTION

This book is intended for those who are at the beginning or near the beginning of their college or graduate school careers. Our goal is to see Christian students embrace a uniquely kingdom vision for their educational experience. Yet, if you are not a follower of Jesus Christ, we believe there is a lot of helpful material in this text for you as well. This season of life provides an opportunity to develop some skills that will help equip you to be successful in your education and career. We want to help you be intentional about this time in your life. The approach to education and skills we discuss in this book can help you through your studies and wherever God leads you.

The Gospel Explained

Perhaps it would be helpful to explain what we mean when we say someone is a Christian or follower of Christ.[1] Put simply, a Christian is someone who follows Jesus Christ and the teachings of the Bible. The Bible begins and ends with a picture of God in relationship with people. We are made to be in relationship with God. Christians believe there is one God who made the world and all that is in it. God, the Creator, is a holy God. In other words, he is

---

[1] A helpful, brief text on this topic is Greg Gilbert, *What Is the Gospel?* (Wheaton, IL: Crossway, 2010).

completely righteous and pure. When Adam and Eve—humanity's shared parents—sinned, their relationship with God was severed, and the world itself was broken (Genesis 3; Rom 8:19–22). In many ways, the story of the Bible is about God making things right again.

The Bible teaches that not only did Adam and Eve sin, but so has every person who has ever lived, except one. We'll get to him in a moment. Romans 3:23 says, "For all have sinned and fall short of the glory of God." Sin is disobedience to God. Sin includes things like lying, adultery, or murder, but also lustful or prideful thoughts or even neglecting to do what God has called us to do. Any time we fall short of what God desires for us, we sin. The penalty for our sin is death. Romans 6:23 says, "For the wages of sin is death, but the gift of God is eternal life in Christ Jesus our Lord." So, every person sins, and each sin earns eternal death.[2] We were certainly in a desperate situation, but remember God made us for relationship with him.

So, while we were in a hopeless situation (Rom 5:6), God sent his Son Jesus to die in our place. The last part of Rom 6:23 says "the gift of God is eternal life in Christ Jesus our Lord." The Bible teaches that Jesus came to the earth as a man and lived a sinless life. Since he never sinned, he did not owe the penalty for sin like the rest of us. Because of his great love for us, however, he willingly died on the cross for our sin. Three days later, he was raised from the dead, and now he reigns in heaven with God the Father. Jesus's sinless life, death, and resurrection are what makes salvation possible for all who would call upon him. This is the good news (gospel) of salvation.

Romans 6 reminds us that salvation is offered as a gift. We do not do anything to earn salvation, but we must receive it. The proper response to the gospel is repentance and faith. Repentance simply means we turn from our sin and confess it to God. Faith is the means by which salvation comes. Ephesians 2:8–9 says, "For

---

[2] Notice how "death" is contrasted with "eternal life" in the verse.

you are saved by grace through faith, and this is not from yourselves; it is God's gift—not from works, so that no one can boast." God has graciously and freely made salvation available to those who would call upon him in faith and commit themselves to Jesus. The Bible instructs us to confess Jesus as Lord, believing in our hearts that he was raised from the dead so we can be saved (Rom 10:9–10). Confessing Jesus as "Lord" means calling upon him to be in control of your life. We turn from our sin, which leads to death, and turn to Jesus, who leads to life.

Becoming a follower of Jesus is just the beginning of the Christian life. God intends for us to grow in our relationship with him daily and to help draw others into this relationship as well. Believers are called to kingdom living. God intends for us to live in this world for his glory. Ephesians 2:10 says it this way: "For we are his workmanship, created in Christ Jesus for good works, which God prepared ahead of time for us to do."

In many ways, this book is intended to help followers of Christ understand that their lives are intended for the kingdom's good and not just their own. If you are a follower of Christ, your experience as a student is not simply for you. Your desire should be to seek the Lord and ask what he wants to accomplish in this season of your life.

If you are not yet a follower of Christ, our prayer is that you would consider the teachings of the Bible and come to know Jesus as your Savior. Find a family member or friend you know who is a believer and talk to them about how you can become a follower of Jesus.[3] Read the Bible for yourself and see what it says. But even if you are not ready to do that now, this book can be useful to you. The skills we outline in this work are not just for believers. Everyone can benefit from growing in these areas.

---

[3] If you don't know who to talk to, let us know! We would love to talk with you about following Jesus.

Overview of This Book

The first chapter of this work will lay out our approach to education. In short, if God has called you into a season of education, he has things you should learn now that will be useful for the rest of your life. The following chapters describe a skill that can be developed while you are gaining your education and then provide some practical steps to improve yourself in that skill. We discuss scholarship, productivity, leadership, and relationships. Our prayer is that God will use this text to help you focus on how this season of your life can be used to prepare you for success in life, particularly in service to his kingdom.

Kingdom Education

Glorifying God and serving others is the calling of all those who are in Jesus's kingdom. Jesus's call for us to follow him is a call to join his kingdom. Jesus's first words in the book of Mark are "The time is fulfilled, and the kingdom of God has come near. Repent and believe the good news" (Mark 1:15). The Gospels tell the story of Jesus defeating death through his resurrection and then ascending to heaven where he takes his place at God's right hand as the ruler of all things. Jesus invites all who would participate in his victory over sin and death to profess him as King and begin living now under his reign.[1] Living under the reign of Jesus affects your entire life, and your education is no different. If you are a member

---

[1] If this is not the way you have thought of the invitation Jesus issues his followers, we would invite you to consider how the Bible makes this argument. A good guide to seeing how the Bible is focused on Jesus as King is N. T. Wright, *Simply Good News: Why the Gospel Is News and What Makes It Good* (New York: HarperCollins, 2015). For an in-depth study of how all of Scripture is pointing toward the kingship of Jesus, check out Thomas Schreiner, *The King in His Beauty: A Biblical Theology of the Old and New Testaments* (Grand Rapids: Baker, 2013).

of Jesus's kingdom and pursuing academic work as a student, then you should pursue your academic work as a kingdom student.

Throughout this book, when we use the term "kingdom students," we mean students who view their education as contributing to the work God is calling them to do as a part of Jesus's kingdom. Whether or not you are living under Jesus's lordship, though, the skills we discuss in this book will be valuable for you in school and in the work you undertake throughout your life. For kingdom students, this book should have special value because you view this season of education you are undertaking through the lens of your membership in Jesus's kingdom. Christians who view education in such a way realize that the goal of their education is kingdom service—that is, using the gifts God has given you to glorify him and serve others. Put simply, we want you to consider a kingdom-student approach to education because this helps you become the kingdom servant God is calling you to be.

During your time pursuing an academic degree, God is giving you an opportunity to hone the gifts he has given you through your education. As a Christian student, you must understand that regardless of your background, major, GPA, or intended vocation, a major function of this time in your life is to prepare to serve God's people. You may or may not be preparing for what some Christians call "vocational ministry," meaning a career as a minister, missionary, or pastor; but you are definitely called to kingdom service. If God has called you to pursue higher education, then he intends for this education to help your service in his kingdom.

Becoming a servant may not be why you began your educational pursuits. Often we understand education to be about power, success, and wealth. Recent trends in university and college recruiting tactics further such a view of education. When you chose your current educational path, you likely received information from the school about its job placement rates and the ability to make more money throughout your career if you chose a particular program. Many colleges and universities seek to share these statistics with you so that you can see the value of their degrees.

Nothing is wrong with knowing these numbers, but if you are a Christian student, there is a danger in measuring the value of your degree solely by what your degree can do for you. Kingdom students should apply their education to something greater than their own personal gain. For kingdom students, education must be undertaken for the glory of God and the service of his kingdom. Far more important than what your degree can offer you is how your education can better equip you to be a servant in the kingdom of King Jesus.

Christian students are not alone in their desire to use their degrees to serve others. You will find students from across all faith traditions and academic programs who desire to use their degrees for service. For kingdom students, however, an abstract sense of duty to share the gifts you hone through your education is not enough. Kingdom students have an opportunity to use their education to serve others and glorify God.

Education ought to have purpose; after all, degrees of higher learning are not (and should not be) easy to get. Why does anyone want to go through the effort that it takes to do well in school? What is this endeavor really about? If you desire to be a kingdom student, then you will need to take a particular approach to your pursuit of education. You can show up for class, make good grades, and acquire new skills during your educational career and still miss many of the opportunities to foster your ability to glorify God through kingdom service.

This book provides you with both a kingdom-centered approach to education and specific strategies to apply such an approach to your life during your time as a student. Our prayer is that your work as a kingdom student finds its ultimate goal in your kingdom service and that through that service God would bless his people and bring glory to his name.

Education and Kingdom Obedience

If serving the kingdom rather than achieving wealth and status is the chief goal of kingdom students, then we may ask why we have kingdom students at all. In other words, if service to the kingdom is what is important, then why should we spend time in academic preparation? This question is especially pertinent for students who are not preparing to be pastors, ministers, missionaries, or entering some other vocational ministry role. If your highest calling is to glorify God through kingdom service, then why would you go to med school or be an English major? The answer is that God uses educated servants to further the work of the kingdom. In truth, questions about whether our work is ministerial or professional have their origin in a false dichotomy between the sacred and the secular. While today's culture has often taught that there is a sharp divide between secular and sacred, the Bible teaches that all knowledge is the Lord's.[2]

Educated servants of the kingdom are not better than noneducated servants of the kingdom, nor do they deserve higher status or greater recognition. Some of the greatest kingdom servants throughout history and some of the greatest kingdom servants we have encountered in our ministries did not hold any degrees or care much for scholarship. However, some members of Jesus's kingdom are called to hone the gifts and personalities God has given them through a season of education.

The kingdom of Jesus is not dependent on servants with academic credentials. God blesses the kingdom with some servants who are equipped to think deeply about important issues. Such servants may or may not hold bachelor's, master's, or doctoral degrees. You can become a thoughtful Christian without formal education. Many of the best kingdom thinkers had no formal training. People such as Francis of Assisi, Charles Spurgeon, Frederick Douglass, and A. W. Tozer all made significant contributions to the way Christians think but had no formal education. These people

---

[2] See Job 28:28; Ps 24:1; and Prov 2:6–8.

were, however, deep thinkers who studied a wide variety of material in order to better serve the kingdom.

Formal education is not necessary for effective kingdom work, but God's people have long recognized the value of it. A degree is not necessary to become an educated servant of the kingdom in the same way that a car is not necessary to travel across country. Ask a man hitchhiking a great distance if he would like your car. Ask a woman in a remote village trying to glorify God by healing sick children if she would like to go to med school. Formal education may not be a necessity, but when pursued in the correct manner, it is one of the best ways to prepare for kingdom service.

Servants of Jesus's kingdom should understand that there are specific reasons we should be driven to pursue knowledge through education. Understanding specific ways education can affect kingdom service increases our passion for education. We propose three big-picture reasons kingdom students should care about their education.

The Bible Commends Godly Pursuit of Knowledge, Instruction, and Wisdom

The Bible is not silent on the approach God's people are to take to pursuing education. Some Christians understand the Bible as presenting education as a negative or neutral resource for serving God. Reading selective passages in the Bible demonstrates why some Christians feel education is unnecessary or even harmful for living out the Christian life. First, the Bible rarely emphasizes any kind of formal education or mental acumen in the characters God uses to motivate the biblical story. Because the Bible does not emphasize formal education, some Christians assume that God prefers to use uneducated people to do his work. When Christians believe this, it results in either the lack of pursuit of education or (more common in our current context) people who see no connection between their education and their calling to serve God.

Some biblical texts seem to say explicitly that human knowledge and learning are not important. In 1 Cor 1:18–25, Paul exhorts the Corinthians to understand that God's wisdom in sending Jesus to die on the cross is better than human wisdom, which sees the death of Jesus as foolishness. He says,

> For the word of the cross is foolishness to those who are perishing, but it is the power of God to us who are being saved. For it is written, I will destroy the wisdom of the wise, and I will set aside the intelligence of the intelligent. Where is the one who is wise? Where is the teacher of the law? Where is the debater of this age? Hasn't God made the world's wisdom foolish? For since, in God's wisdom, the world did not know God through wisdom, God was pleased to save those who believe through the foolishness of what is preached. For the Jews ask for signs and the Greeks seek wisdom, but we preach Christ crucified, a stumbling block to the Jews and foolishness to the Gentiles. Yet to those who are called, both Jews and Greeks, Christ is the power of God and the wisdom of God, because God's foolishness is wiser than human wisdom, and God's weakness is stronger than human strength.

If God has made the world's wisdom foolish, then isn't pursuing wisdom through earthly education a waste of time? First Corinthians 1:18–25 does demonstrate that earthly wisdom falls far short of God's wisdom in allowing Jesus to die on the cross—so much so that compared to God's wisdom, the world's wisdom is foolishness. This text does not, however, mean that human learning is against God's will, nor does it mean that pursuing education is a worthless endeavor.

When Paul speaks about worldly wisdom, he is not referring to all human learning. Paul is referring to the dominant way of thinking in the world that elevates the powerful, wealthy, and eloquent. By contrast, Jesus, who was humble to the point of crucifixion, is the ultimate manifestation of God's power.[3] Passages such as 1 Cor 1:18–25, therefore, do not diminish the importance of pursuing education and developing the intellect. In fact, John Piper points out that if we do not think seriously about passages like this one, we will not be able to understand them in the first place![4]

The Bible is clear that there is a type of worldly knowledge that is antithetical to the truth of God expressed in the gospel. However, the Bible is not anti-intellectual. Scripture never claims that the pursuit of knowledge for God's glory is wrong. In fact, the Bible provides us with a theology that shows why the pursuit of knowledge is needed and commends us to pursue knowledge.

Consider the words King Solomon speaks to his son in Proverbs:

> My son, if you accept my words and store up my commands within you, listening closely to wisdom and directing your heart to understanding; furthermore, if you call out to insight and lift your voice to understanding, if you seek it like silver and search for it like hidden treasure, then you will understand the fear of the LORD and discover the knowledge of God. For the LORD gives wisdom; from his mouth come knowledge and understanding. (2:1–6)

These inspired words of Scripture make it clear that there is such a thing as pursuit of knowledge, wisdom, and understanding that is to be greatly desired by the people of God! Notice that wisdom, knowledge, and understanding are gifts from the Lord; thus, our ability to obtain these characteristics is a gracious gift from God.

While the Bible makes clear that the ability to pursue knowledge is a gift, that pursuit is also complicated by our sin. The pursuit of knowledge cannot heal the sinfulness of our world, but the

---

[3] See Alan F. Johnson, *1 Corinthians*, The IVP New Testament Commentary Series 7 (Downers Grove, IL: InterVarsity Press, 2004), 54–59.

[4] John Piper, *Think* (Wheaton, IL: Crossway, 2010), 154.

sinfulness of our world has corrupted our pursuit of knowledge. Paul states in 1 Tim 6:5 that one of the reasons false doctrines are taught in churches is that the minds of those who teach them are "depraved and deprived of the truth." We are blessed to pursue knowledge through the life of the mind, but our minds are corrupt tools for this endeavor.

In his mercy, God renews believers' corrupt minds so that we can discern the will of God. Paul tells us in Rom 12:1–2,

> Therefore, brothers and sisters, in view of the mercies of God, I urge you to present your bodies as a living sacrifice, holy and pleasing to God; this is your true worship. Do not be conformed to this age, but be transformed by the renewing of your mind, so that you may discern what is the good, pleasing, and perfect will of God.

Notice that our minds are not restored without reason. God graciously renews our minds as we internalize his Word and obey it so that we might "discern what is the good, pleasing, and perfect will of God." God has redeemed our minds for the purpose of discerning his will so that we might please him. God has redeemed our minds so that his people—both at the individual and corporate levels—can live lives of true worship. If those in Jesus's kingdom are to partake in this true worship, they must seek the renewing of their minds and put their renewed minds to use in discerning God's will.

The Nature of the Christian Faith Demands Careful Thought

Some of the smartest people in the world are not Christians, and some of the dumbest people in the world are Christians. Some of the smartest people in the world are Christians, and some of the dumbest people in the world are not Christians. Both of the previous sentences are true. Christianity is no respecter of intellect—the brilliant and the simple are called to the kingdom, and they enter on equal footing. Jesus made it clear that intellect is not what makes someone mighty in the kingdom of God. In Luke 10, when Jesus's followers return to him with incredible reports of what God has done in their missionary journey, Luke tells us, "At that time [Jesus] rejoiced in the Holy Spirit and said, 'I praise you, Father, Lord of heaven and earth, because you have hidden these things from the wise and intelligent and revealed them to infants. Yes, Father, because this was your good pleasure'" (Luke 10:21). Jesus is making the point to his followers that their success is not due to their wisdom and intelligence, but to God's grace.

All are called to come into the kingdom of God; within that kingdom, some are called to equip God's people to think in a way that glorifies God. Christians are not required to have tremendous intelligence, yet understanding and explaining some elements of the Christian faith requires careful thought. What we mean by this is that, even though intelligence and careful thought do not make you a better Christian, some elements of the Christian faith require intelligent and carefully thought-out explanations.

Consider as an example the trinitarian nature of the Christian faith. *The New City Catechism*, which I (Cory) and my wife use with our children, asks the question, "How many persons are there in God?"[5] Before we even discuss the complicated nature of the answer to this question, let's examine the complicated nature of the question itself. How do we define the word "persons"? Why are a group of people who believe in one all-powerful God asking this question? The question itself is complicated and worthy of serious thought. The answer is even more complicated: "There are three persons in the one true and living God: the Father, the Son, and the Holy Spirit. They are the same in substance, equal in power and glory."[6] How can three distinct persons be equal in substance? If God is three persons, how is he one? Christians have struggled with this issue for millennia, yet the Trinity is so essential to the

---

[5] *The New City Catechism: 52 Questions & Answers for Our Hearts & Minds* (Wheaton, IL: Crossway, 2017), 21.

[6] *New City Catechism*, 21.

Christian faith that it is question number three of fifty-two in a catechism geared toward children!

When my (Norris's) oldest daughter was young, she was especially talkative at bedtime as many children are. I'm certain that much of this was about being able to stay up a few minutes later, but nightly conversations would often veer to unexpected places. One night she said, "I love Jesus!"

"That's good honey," I replied.

"I love God, too!"

"That's good," I replied.

Then she said, "But aren't Jesus and God the same person? How can Jesus pray to God? How can God send his Son Jesus and yet they are the same people?" It was like a stream of deep theological questions all at once. Finally, she threw up her hands and said, "This is so confusing to me!"

Since she was pretty young, and I wanted her to go to sleep soon, I think my reply was something like, "It's confusing to a lot of adults too. Good night." Over time, though, we have been able to think more deeply about the nature of the triune God. Still, anyone who has thought long about the Trinity has felt like throwing his hands up in great confusion.

Here is some good news: you don't have to understand everything about the Trinity to be a Christian. Here is more good news: God invites us to struggle to understand the Trinity because we have the opportunity to glorify him in this struggle and come to know him more completely. If we are to partake in the blessing of struggling to understand the Trinity, then we need to train our minds to think. If others in the kingdom are to partake in this God-glorifying act, then they need educated servants—not just pastors and theologians, but lay leaders capable of serious thought—to lead them in this activity.[7]

---

[7] We raise a lot of questions about the Trinity in this section, but do not give answers because that is not the purpose of this book. If you have additional questions about the Trinity, you can check out

Another example of the complex nature of Christianity is deciding which books make up the Christian Bible. The word "Bible" is deceivingly complex. The Bible is composed of sixty-six books that came together over hundreds of years. Nowhere in Scripture do we find a story about how God delivered the Bible to his people on golden tablets. The Bible came together over time as God made clear to his people which books contain his authoritative words. This in no way diminishes the authority of the Bible. The Bible is without error and is the absolute authority for all Christian doctrine and practice, but that does not mean the Bible has a simple history—far from it!

The content of the Christian Bible is also complex. The Bible is not a step-by-step instructional manual for Christians. Instead, the Bible is a collection of stories, poems, songs, letters, prophecies, parables, and other types of literature. Through these diverse literary genres God reveals his will to us and invites us to participate in the story of his people revealed in Scripture. Reading the Bible requires serious thought. Serious thought requires serious thinkers.

The two examples we offer above are just a fraction of the ways in which Christianity is a complex faith. Christianity does not require followers to be intelligent, but the kingdom must have servants who are capable of thinking about the complex ways in which God has revealed himself and who lead others to do the same. If God's people lack such leaders, the consequences are disastrous.[8]

---

the following resources: Fred Sanders, *The Triune God*, New Studies in Dogmatics (Grand Rapids: Zondervan, 2016); R. C. Sproul, *What Is the Trinity?*, Crucial Questions Series 10 (Orlando, FL: Reformation Trust, 2011).

[8] Mark Noll wrote an excellent book that outlines how evangelical Christians have devalued intellectual life; it gives some guidelines for how we can come to value intellectual pursuits in evangelical Christianity. Mark Noll, *The Scandal of the Evangelical Mind* (Grand Rapids: Eerdmans, 1994).

The Complicated World in Which We Live Requires Careful Thought

We have chosen to call the Christian faith complex and the world in which we live complicated. If you examine dictionary entries for the words "complicated" and "complex," you will find that the definitions of the two words are largely the same, yet we mean something distinct in our use of them in this book. When we say the Christian faith is complex, we mean that parts of Christianity are, by their nature, vast and interconnected. When we say the world is complicated, we mean both that it is, by its nature, complex and that it is also complicated as a result of the sinful, fallen state of the people who inhabit it. The world is complicated because it is not the way it is supposed to be; Christianity is complex because it tells us the way things ought to be and will be.

People may argue over the solutions to the world's problems, but they are likely to agree that the problems facing the world are complicated. The complicated nature of the world's problems divides us at many levels. The world struggles with racial discrimination, sexual slavery, environmental abuse, and war. Some of these problems seem to have straightforward solutions; however, if you take time to think through these issues, you will find they are more complicated than you assumed.

Recently I (Cory) drove through an area where the landscape was ravaged due to coal mining. As I drove, I began to lament the failure of humanity to work and guard creation as God commanded us. Then I drove to my house and turned on my lights, turned down my thermostat, and plugged in my laptop and my cell phone—all of which are connected to a power grid fueled in part by coal. I believe that abusing the good creation God has given us is sinful. I also realize that the reason people harm the earth in such a way is that people like me pay them to do it every time we pay a power bill. If I want to be a part of a solution to this problem, I need to recognize that the things in life I use and enjoy every day are part of the reason the problem exists.

My story illustrates that the problems we face in our world are complicated. Such complications are problematic for all people but present a particular challenge for the people seeking to live as kingdom citizens. Christians must develop an understanding of the complicated world in which we live and also an understanding of how our faith informs our approach to that world. The way in which Christians ought to approach the world is often referred to as a "Christian worldview." When we consider the complicated nature of our world, we find that forming a Christian worldview is not a simple task.

We live in a world filled with challenging concerns. Abortion, immigration, religious freedom, racial tensions, issues of gender and sexuality, approaches to war and peace, and countless other emotionally, politically, and spiritually-charged problems are present in our world. Christians cannot avoid these issues, nor should we! If Christians do not speak to these most crucial issues, then we will fail to equip God's people to glorify God as they encounter them. Members of the kingdom called to pursue education should be prepared to discuss complicated issues—especially those in their field of study—in a way that glorifies God and edifies fellow believers.

As Christians approach controversial and complicated realities, they must be careful to avoid adopting the world's positions on how to think about them. The Bible makes clear that Christians are to have a unique approach to the world in which they live. The apostle Paul reminded the Roman believers—who also lived in a complicated world—"Do not be conformed to this age, but be transformed by the renewing of your mind, so that you may discern what is the good, pleasing, and perfect will of God" (Rom 12:2). God's command to his people in Rom 12:2 mandates that we have a unique approach to interacting with the complicated world in which we live. The people of God have a responsibility to discern God's will rather than follow the whims of culture.

Discerning the will of God in a complicated world is a difficult task. The reality is that Christians, particularly American evangelicals, often struggle to take the careful time and effort necessary to discern God's will. Mark Noll noted that evangelical Christianity is "a culture where intense, detailed, and precise efforts have been made to understand the Bible. But it is not a culture where the same effort has been expended to understand the world or, even more important, the processes by which wisdom from Scripture should be brought into relation with knowledge about the world."[9] The failure of evangelical Christians to discern the "good, pleasing, and perfect will of God" in the midst of a complicated culture is due, in part, to a lack of educated kingdom servants.

The shortage of educated kingdom servants does not come from an absence of Christians with academic degrees. Instead, the shortage comes primarily from the way Christians separate the knowledge and skills they acquire in their educational pursuits from their roles as servants of the kingdom. We need people who have been granted the opportunity for education to bring their full selves to their involvement in kingdom work. They must become educated servants, serving God by sharing what God has taught them with his people. If Christians are to discern God's will for living in this complicated world, then we need fellow citizens of the kingdom to guide us in understanding how God's Word informs our approach to the complicated issues of the world.

Every Christian should be committed to learning the Word of God, but those who feel called to pastoral ministry have a particular responsibility to dedicate themselves to a quality theological education. All Christians should be concerned about the education of their children, but those who are called into the vocation of education have a particular responsibility to dedicate themselves to the study of their own craft—not just for the sake of their careers or the children in their classrooms, but also so they can help their fellow Christians understand God's will for education. Christian doctors and scientists have a responsibility to help fellow Christians discern how to approach the many complicated issues that arise from their fields. Kingdom computer programmers have a responsibility to

---

[9] Noll, *Scandal*, 15.

help Christians discern God's will for how his people implement technology. The kingdom will thrive when every one of its members lays their academic pursuit at the feet of their Lord Jesus Christ and says, "Use what you have given me to accomplish the mission of your kingdom!"

Kingdom Students and the Church

This book is meant to be a practical guide for students, not a theological treatise, so we won't give a full theology of why the church is the primary organization for kingdom service.[10] However, if you have not thought about the necessity of the church in your life as a Christian, we challenge you to look at how central the church is to the story of the New Testament. The earliest Christians came together for worship and ministry. The book of Acts tells us how this group went out into the Roman Empire proclaiming the message of Jesus's resurrection. Wherever the apostles went, they equipped new converts to function as a church. Paul's letters were all written to churches or leaders in churches. The book of Revelation opens with messages to the churches in Asia. As a biblical Christian, your primary arena for kingdom service should be the church.

Many students express a desire to love and serve God but don't believe that their relationship to the church is necessary for such work. A common refrain among many students is "I love God, but not the church." This view is understandable. The church is an imperfect institution filled with imperfect people who do imperfect things—sometimes hurtful and evil things. But though the desire to bypass the church in your service to God is understandable, it is an unacceptable way to approach your work as a follower of Jesus.

---

[10] If you want a more detailed introduction to what the church is and why her ministries are the primary outlet for Christians, see Mark Dever, *9 Marks of a Healthy Church*, 3rd ed. (Wheaton, IL: Crossway, 2013); and Jonathan Leeman, *Church Membership: How the World Knows Who Represents Jesus* (Wheaton, IL: Crossway, 2012).

The main reason for this is the witness of Scripture as we referenced above. But we also want to challenge you to consider what is at the root of the idea of bypassing the church as you seek to serve God. The church is made up of women and men who are being sanctified by the work of the Holy Spirit but are still capable of being hurtful and foolish. The church is composed of people like me . . . and of people like you. Trying to go around the church as you seek to serve God will not save you from the problems of working with sinners; you will take all those problems with you because you are a sinner too.

The Special Opportunity of Higher Education

Kingdom students need to have a unique understanding of education. Education is more than a degree. God is good to create us with the capacity to learn throughout our lives. Learning opportunities come to us in the form of wise counsel from others and learning through various life situations, in and out of a formal education environment. Our target audience for this work, however, is students who are pursuing formal education and, therefore, need to understand the unique opportunities to learn in their educational experience.

Whether you are enrolled in undergraduate or graduate work, your life takes on a certain structure as a student. Students who are living on or near the campuses where they are pursuing their degrees often find that almost every aspect of their daily lives is affected by their choice to pursue academic work. If you are a kingdom student, you understand that the entirety of the life experiences you undergo as a student present opportunities for you to learn to be a better servant of the kingdom.

The daily rhythms of life as a student provide a time to hone skills that are essential for becoming a lifelong, effective kingdom servant. Regardless of their majors or the careers for which they are preparing, students can develop life skills in a controlled environment and receive constructive feedback from their professors and classmates about their ability to use these skills. Some of the skills you can strengthen in your education are those directly addressed in the curriculum you intend to study. Whether you are in school to become a mechanical engineer, missionary, nurse, or social studies teacher, you have an opportunity to immerse yourself in the study of skills associated with that trade. These skills will be honed by passionate pursuit of knowledge in your classes and the work associated with those classes. You may also have chances to dialogue with your professors and professionals in your field outside of class. Your institution will likely provide resources through libraries, laboratories, and electronic databases that put knowledge needed to master your craft at your fingertips. If you are to be a kingdom student, you must make much of these opportunities. You must also realize that these are not the only prospects for learning that God gives you in this season of education.

Kingdom students must understand that the goal of education is not merely knowledge but wisdom. Readers of the book of Proverbs find that wisdom is not just knowledge; wisdom is the ability to do what ought to be done. This means we can learn wisdom not only from brilliant instructors, but also from things as simple as ants. Proverbs 6:6 challenges lazy people: "Go to the ant, you slacker! Observe its ways and become wise." Wisdom does not just come from lectures and reading, but also from careful observation of the world in which God has placed us. If you are to be a servant of the kingdom, then you must seek wisdom in your education, and this wisdom must be gleaned both inside and outside of the classroom.

In this book, we invite you into a kingdom approach to education that prepares you to serve God's people. Learning how to prepare for kingdom service through your coursework is certainly a part of a kingdom approach, but proper preparation also involves being intentional about all of the educational opportunities you have in this time of life.

Students are expected to be at certain places at certain times, often on a daily basis. Your success in your classes will depend on your ability to be where you need to be when you need to be there. Students also must learn to balance their educational responsibilities with various other activities and responsibilities in their lives. If you are to succeed at these tasks, you must learn to be productive. Productivity is helpful for success as a student, but being efficient with your time is even more important if you are to be a kingdom servant. Kingdom students must seek to hone productivity skills as they pursue their academic work.

Your education will present you with unique experiences to foster leadership skills. Class projects, campus events, and work with student organizations all present you with opportunities to hone your skills as a leader. Whether or not you feel called to take a position of leadership within a church, you need to give attention to fostering your skills as a leader. One of the best ways to become an effective follower is to have an idea of what effective leadership looks like and how this better serves the kingdom.

Students come into educational work at various stages of life. Whatever your situation in life, you enter into your educational work with family relationships that you must continue to cultivate. Added to those relationships are those that you will form with friends, classmates, professors, and others during your educational career. Success in achieving your educational goals is not always dependent on learning how to cultivate these relationships. Success in serving Jesus's kingdom, however, requires communicating with others. Kingdom students, therefore, must make learning to cultivate relationships a priority.

The remainder of this book is devoted to providing you with practical strategies for developing your ability to serve the church through honing your skills in scholarship, productivity, leadership, and interpersonal relationships during your time as a student. These are not all the areas of life where students have the opportunity to develop godly wisdom during their studies, but they are the areas that are most naturally developed during one's time as a student and are most needed for service to the church. Kingdom students are challenged to implement the strategies outlined in the following chapters so that they might become better servants of God's kingdom.

The Cost of a Kingdom Approach to Education

Before moving into more practical areas of this book, we do want to issue a word of warning. Kingdom education does not come cheap. All higher education comes at a cost. In most circumstances there is a financial cost involved in the pursuit of education. In all cases, education requires a tremendous sacrifice of time and effort. If you seek to be a kingdom student, however, you will need to consider additional costs.

Adopting a kingdom approach to education will change the way you approach higher education. In American culture, the time you spend as a student—particularly at the undergraduate level—is often seen as the last respite from adulthood. College students have a reputation for sleeping late, indulging in leisure activities, and focusing the majority of their attention on doing what they want to do during the last hurrah before the responsibility of adult life arrives post-graduation. If you are to be a kingdom student, you must leave this "me-centered" approach to education behind you.

Kingdom students do not have to forsake fun—far from it. In the chapters that follow, many of the strategies we suggest will increase your enjoyment of your education. The ultimate goal of a kingdom student, however, cannot be self-gratification. Self-gratification is too small a goal. Kingdom students must pursue education out of love for God and the service of others.

A kingdom view of education is the natural outflow of applying Jesus's instruction in the great commandment to your approach to education. When asked what the greatest commandment is, Jesus responded,

> Love the Lord your God with all your heart, with all your soul, and with all your mind. This is the greatest and most important command. The second is like it: Love your neighbor as yourself. All the Law and the Prophets depend on these two commands. (Matt 22:37–40)

To be a kingdom student, you must seek to pursue education out of love for God and love for people. Kingdom students understand that their ultimate goal is not to enjoy themselves in education or become rich and important because of their degrees. Instead, kingdom students count the cost of pursuing education for the sake of loving God and others through service to the kingdom of Jesus.

2

Kingdom Academics

We have established that kingdom students should value education. The next two chapters are all about how to do the academic work that is essential to your education. Whether you are in college or graduate school, you have at least twelve years of educational experience at this point in your life. That is a tremendous amount of experience! In fact, you have likely spent almost as much time in school as you have spent doing anything else. Since this is the case, do you even need to read this part of the book? Shouldn't you be an expert by now?

You probably do need some help developing new skills to succeed as you pursue your degree. That is okay, because few people enter a new degree program with all the skills they need to succeed. Success in your academic work will require building skills for this new level of education.

In high school, most of the work students do is guided work that occurs in the context of a classroom. Your homework was likely limited to things like reading assignments, practice problems, writing assignments, and memorization work. Such tasks will be important for your work in higher education, but you will have to sharpen your skills in these areas and develop new ones in order to succeed.

According to data collected by the United States Census Bureau, only around one-third of adults in the United States hold a bachelor's degree or higher. In contrast, the same data indicate that nine out of ten U.S. adults have a high school diploma.[1] These data demonstrate that achieving a college or graduate degree places you among the top tier of educated people in the country. If these distinguished degrees are actually valuable, they should be challenging to complete and should foster specific skills and knowledge within those who complete them. We want to help you identify the skills you need to succeed academically and develop strategies to hone those skills.

Academic skills matter for any student who desires to be successful in academic work. For kingdom students, however, there are particular reasons to foster academic skills. We have already seen that kingdom students should be interested in thinking deeply about the world in which God has placed them. Beyond being valuable for deep thought about the world, academic skills also have practical applications. Kingdom students should foster such skills, not just because they desire to perform well in class or engage in intellectual musings, but because academic abilities will equip them for good work throughout their entire lives. Not only will these skills benefit you in future work, they also will equip you to live out a consistent Christian witness while pursuing your degree.

Academic Excellence Equips You for a Lifetime of Good Work

You may imagine that your future career will look very different from your time in college or graduate school. Though your daily life will likely change in many ways once you complete your degree, many of the skills that you develop as a student will enable you to excel at your profession after graduation.

---

[1] https://www.census.gov/library/publications/2016/demo/p20 -578.html, accessed July 23, 2019.

Have you ever wondered what value organizations find in hiring college graduates? For some vocations, the connection between an academic degree and a specific job opportunity is obvious. Those who wish to work in nursing must have a degree in nursing because they need specialized training for that field. But why is it that many companies require a college degree from any major as a prerequisite for being hired in a given job? One of the main reasons for such hiring practices is that those who have gone through advanced academic work should have some specialized skills that are valuable in all contexts. Employees with advanced academic degrees *should* have the ability to process information efficiently, communicate clearly, and think critically as a result of their academic work. Whether you are working in retail sales, the service industry, a Fortune 500 company, or any other vocation, sharp academic skills will allow you to excel in many areas of your job.

One of the first people I (Cory) saw demonstrate the value of a college education was a woman with whom I worked in a hardware store when I was in high school. She was finishing her degree at a nearby college, and the effect her education had on her work was noticeable even though her degree had nothing to do with selling hardware. When the internet went down, slowing our ability to look up parts for customers, she didn't call the service provider. She read the information on the bottom of the router and used it to fix the internet service. Once, a customer came in disgruntled over a misunderstanding about some charges on a receipt, and she was able to explain the charges to satisfy the customer. If we needed to write an email to a customer, detailing a quote for a large order, she was the natural choice to write the email because she understood how to provide all the relevant details without making the quote difficult to understand. This woman's degree was not in management or sales, yet her education made her a valuable employee. She moved on to higher-paying jobs; but as long as she wanted to stay at the hardware store, the managers were glad to have her and would pay her as much as they could justify to keep her employed there.

This story illustrates how even in work that may seem to have no connection to academic tasks, academic skills are useful. If this is the case in a hardware store, how much more valuable will these skills be if you pursue a career directly related to your field of study? Your goal for completing an academic degree should not be to receive a piece of paper that allows you to get a job in your field. Your goal should be to develop skills and acquire knowledge that allows you to excel at the work to which God calls you.

Academic Excellence Is a Witness of Commitment to Kingdom Service

I (Cory) teach students from multiple academic disciplines who have varying levels of commitment to serving Jesus's kingdom. One of the things that drives me crazy is that there is not always a correlation between students who are serious about their Christian faith and students being serious about their academic work. Many Christian students see no connection between their professed faith and the effort they put toward their studies. Non-Christian students in their classes sometimes notice this lack of effort. When Christian students fail to put forth effort in their academic work, they are sending a message to others that the degree God has called them to pursue is not worth their best effort. What a poor approach to faithful service in the kingdom of Jesus!

I (Norris) teach at New Orleans Baptist Theological Seminary. One of the things that baffles me is students who have moved their families in order to follow the call of God on their lives but who refuse to give their best efforts in the classroom. These students have demonstrated their willingness to sacrifice for God's call, but they disconnect the classroom from their obedience. Sometimes students fail to see that God's call upon their lives to school at this moment requires their diligent effort.

Please understand, both of us have failed to be faithful in multiple areas of our lives, and the classroom is no exception. One of us (Cory) even failed a class in college. Our desire is not to tell poor students that they are also poor Christians; instead, we desire to challenge Christian students to understand their academic work as an opportunity to illustrate the fruit of kingdom service. Here are a few ways that academic excellence increases your ability for kingdom service:

1. *A commitment to academic excellence should testify to God's design in leading you to your studies.* Christians understand that we live in a world where God is in charge and where he takes particular pleasure in ordering the lives of those who follow him. Psalm 37:23 reminds us, "A person's steps are established by the LORD, and he takes pleasure in his way." If you believe that God has been pleased to lead you to a particular area of study that requires a particular class, then your performance in that class should be a testimony to this truth.

2. *A commitment to academic excellence should demonstrate a commitment to serving others.* For kingdom students, the increased ability to serve others should always factor into their education. Consider students who are pursuing degrees in nursing. Don't you want future nurses to fulfill their studies with excellence? When you get a shot, you should certainly hope the person administering it paid attention in his classes! If engineering students don't pursue excellence in their studies, how can they serve others by building secure bridges? If accounting majors don't devote themselves to learning all they can in the classroom, how will they be able to serve people who trust them to manage their money? Kingdom students understand that one of the primary reasons God calls us to learn is so that we can be better servants in the kingdom of Jesus. The more dedicated we are to the things we learn, the more capable we will be to accomplish the good work God has for us.

3. *A commitment to academic excellence should flow from your wonder of God's creation.* An old hymn proclaims, "This is

my Father's world, He shines in all that's fair; / In the rustling grass I hear Him pass, He speaks to me everywhere!"[2] These words remind Christians that God reveals himself in all things he has created. The Bible reminds us that God's revelation of himself in creation is so clear that it leaves his creatures with no excuse for wicked actions that do not align themselves with God's holy nature: "For his invisible attributes, that is, his eternal power and divine nature, have been clearly seen since the creation of the world, being understood through what he has made. As a result, people are without excuse" (Rom 1:20). When we think of how our studies cause us to feel awe in the world God has created, we likely think of the natural sciences—biology, geology, etc. Science does provide an enormous opportunity to consider God's creative work, but so do all other disciplines! God is good to create humans with a unique ability to communicate. When we study language, literature, and grammar, we should marvel at the possibilities of expression God has granted his creatures. Students of music will realize that notes and scales were not created by previous musicians. They were discovered—that is, they simply have come to describe how God created sound to function.

4. *A commitment to academic excellence should be driven by a desire to become a better reader of God's Word.* God is gracious to do far more than just speak to us through the natural world. God speaks to us in an even more direct way by giving us the Bible. One of the great opportunities education presents for kingdom students is the ability to become better readers of the Bible as a result of their educational pursuits. This does not apply just for

---

[2] Franklin L. Shepard, "This Is My Father's World," in *The Baptist Hymnal* (Nashville: Convention Press, 1956), 59.

students who are majoring in ministry or Christian studies or are taking a course on the Bible.[3] In whatever class you take, your commitment to excellence in that class can lead you to become a better reader of the biblical text. Math classes help develop critical thinking skills that can aid you in thinking deeply about complex biblical issues. Communications courses teach you the theory of communication, which equips you to better understand how God communicates through the Bible. Each class that has a reading assignment builds in you an ability to read for comprehension. Please understand that this is not a call for you to see every class as an illustration for how to understand the Bible. Instead, we want you to see that every class can give you additional tools and skills that can help you better understand the Bible and better apply what it says. Here is what we know for sure: you will never be a better student of the Bible because you failed to work toward academic excellence in a course.

All four of the reasons we discussed above concern how commitment to academic excellence produces valuable results in your life and your service to others. Ultimately, however, your greatest reason for pursuing academic excellence should not be about producing anything. As a member of Jesus's kingdom, your greatest reason for pursuing academic excellence is obedience to King Jesus.

Consider Paul's words in Col 3:17: "And whatever you do, in word or in deed, do everything in the name of the Lord Jesus, giving thanks to God the Father through him." Notice the motivation the Bible gives for doing any activity. Members of Jesus's

---

[3] If you are taking a course on the Bible and especially if you are majoring in Christian studies, ministry, doing a seminary degree, etc., you need to know that growing in your knowledge of the Bible is one of the most (and maybe the most) important goals you have in your education.

kingdom are to speak and act "in the name of the Lord Jesus." For Christians, our ultimate motivation for any work is that we do it as representatives of Jesus—to glorify him through the things we say and do.

On one hand, pursuing academic excellence as a member of Jesus's kingdom should stir in us a sense of responsibility for our academic work. If you are a kingdom student, then your effort in your studies should be for the glory of Jesus. Coasting through your responsibilities by avoiding the hard work of being a student wherever possible is a failure to be a faithful member of Jesus's kingdom. Kingdom students should understand that more is on the line with their academic work than just grades and degrees.

On the other hand, pursuing academic excellence as a member of Jesus's kingdom should alleviate a great deal of stress. The measure of kingdom students' academic success is not found in the grades they make or the awards they receive; it is in their obedience to King Jesus through putting forth their best effort in their academic work. God did not create all of us with the same abilities. You may find that you exert all the talent and intellect God has given you, and you do not make an A in all your classes. Do not be discouraged! For kingdom students, success is measured by obedience, not GPA. Each of us can think of students who have worked hard and earned C's while others have gained A's without having to give their best efforts. The students who have taken their education seriously are the ones we are most grateful for, and ultimately those students will be more likely to succeed after school is finished.

One of the things both of us have found in our careers is there are scholars who are far more gifted than we are. If you look us up on Google, you will find that we are not famous authors or world-renowned lecturers. God has gifted both of us with intellectual gifts according to the work he has called us to do, but neither of us could be described as a genius. The measure of our success, however, is not how we match up to other people. We have learned that comparing ourselves with others can lead to pride or self-doubt, but we are at our best and happiest when we remember that the measure of our success is obedience to King Jesus. Trust us, measuring your success based on faithfulness to Jesus rather than faithfulness to the world's systems of success (sometimes, even the measures of grade point average) is a liberating thing.

3

A Strategy for Kingdom Academics

We hope you are convinced that academic excellence equips you for your work as a servant of Jesus's kingdom. But believing academic excellence is important—even for the good reasons we laid out in previous chapters—is not enough. No one is capable of being a great student just by caring about his or her schoolwork. The desire to be a good student should lead you to act on that desire. Now you must learn and master skills that will equip you to pursue excellence in your academic work.

The matters we discuss next are presented in the same order in which you will encounter material in most of your classes.[1] When you come into a class, you will receive a syllabus and other course materials. In these materials you will find the reading and lecture

---

[1] We considered including a section on class attendance. Perhaps nothing will affect your ability to succeed more than simply showing up on time and being ready for class. We decided that we couldn't write a full section about showing up to class; but by all means, make it a habit to attend class on time.

schedule for the semester. You will be tested on the material you encounter in lectures and in your readings.[2] Each of these stages of a course requires a particular set of skills.

Using the Course Syllabus

One of the differences between high school classes and classes in higher education is that learning in college and graduate courses is self-driven. In K-12 education, teachers help students build the structure they need for learning by giving them time in class to do assignments and readings, spending class periods reviewing for exams, and reminding students (and maybe even their parents) of upcoming assignments and exams. Some college professors use similar methods to help their students; but in most college courses, your professors will take a more hands-off approach to your study habits. You may think that not guiding you through the details of a course comes from a lack of concern for your success, but this is not the case. The reason professors do not micromanage your academic work is that they are treating you like an adult rather than a child.

Because you are now learning as an adult student, your professors will not hold your hand through every action you take in the class. Instead, they will provide you with the relevant information you need to know to succeed in the course. The document that contains the information you need to know for each course is called a syllabus.

The word "syllabus" comes from the Greek word for "list." Essentially, that is what a course syllabus is—a list of all the things you need to know to succeed in the class. The syllabus tells you vital

---

[2] Another major component of many courses is writing research papers. Developing as a writer requires reading an entire book on the topic, and there are several good ones available. In addition to the style guide required by your school or academic discipline, we recommend C. M. Gill, *Essential Writing Skills for College and Beyond* (Cincinnati, OH: Writer's Digest Books, 2014).

pieces of information such as where a class meets, what textbook you need to buy, and how your grade in the course will be calculated. In college and graduate school, every class will have a syllabus.

Some professors forget that using a syllabus is a new skill to first-year students and may even forget to remind you that there is a syllabus for the course, though it is likely posted online. Whether or not your professor reviews the syllabus with you, you must review it yourself. If the professor did not tell you where to find the syllabus, ask her where you can access it. By the end of your first week of classes, you should have reviewed the syllabus for each of your courses.

Syllabi (that is, more than one syllabus) take some skill to read because they serve multiple purposes. They are used to communicate relevant information to you as a student, but they are also used by your school to communicate that each class meets a certain standard. A twelve-page syllabus may only have three pages you really need to review to know the essential information for the course. We encourage you to focus your attention on the areas below in addition to any other items a professor may call to your attention:

1. *Professor's information.* Your syllabus should list your professor's contact information and office hours, usually near the top. Knowing how to contact your professor is vital to success in a course. If you have a question about an assignment, you need to contact the professor using the information provided. Some issues may even require a meeting with the professor. Your professor should be available to meet with you in the office hours listed on the syllabus. In some circumstances, a professor may want you to contact a teaching assistant (TA) about certain issues. If so, the syllabus will contain the TA's contact information and/or office hours as well.

    Do not be afraid to ask your professor in or out of class for clarification. Not every professor will welcome additional contact, even though we believe they should. However, most professors will be excited that you care

The main reason you must learn to read your syllabi is so that you can know what it takes to succeed in all of your classes. Another reason is that the skill of reading a syllabus gets you ready for learning how to do specific tasks and jobs in your future work. If you get a job out of college and are handed a manual for your position, you need to be able to read the manual and know what is expected of you in your new role. Knowing how to read a syllabus lays a foundation for reading such material.

Taking Lecture Notes

Most college and graduate school courses have a significant lecture component. The professor will guide the students by talking about the course material and guiding class discussion. The length of a lecture depends on the format of the course, but lectures typically last at least fifty minutes. Suppose your professor speaks at the average rate of 150 words per minute (wpm).[3] This means that over the course of a fifty-minute lecture she would present you with 7,500 words' worth of information. If your professor lectures three times a week, she presents you with 22,500 words per week, which means that on your midterm you are accountable for 180,000 words, and 360,000 words' worth of information on the final exam! If you are going to remember all the relevant information from class lectures, you will need to take notes.

Taking class notes promotes active listening during a lecture. Active listening engages you in the process of hearing a lecture. Have you ever been in a class when a teacher was speaking and wondered to yourself, *What am I supposed to be doing?* Note-taking eliminates the uncertainty about your role during class. You should

---

[3] The average is according to the National Center for Voice and Speech, http://ncvs.org/e-learning/tutorials/qualities.html, accessed August 1, 2019. The rate of 150 wpm is for conversational speech. The rate for public speaking is typically faster.

be listening for the next relevant points your professor makes during the lecture.

Taking notes in class also provides you with a record of the information from class lectures. We do not remember all the information someone tells us; in fact, some research indicates we may forget as much as 75 percent of what we hear![4] Taking notes provides us with a document for review that helps us remember the relevant data we have forgotten. Notes, therefore, are essential as you prepare for tests in lecture-based courses.

Understanding why note-taking is necessary is not difficult, but learning to take quality notes can be a different story. If you struggle to take quality notes, you are not alone. Many students have never taken notes; they've only copied materials from whiteboards and PowerPoint slides. Taking lecture notes requires more than just copying information.

There are several helpful systems for taking notes well.[5] You may find it helpful to research various note-taking systems and use one or multiple methods yourself. Whether you use a particular note system or develop your own unique system, you will need to take four actions to ensure quality:

1. *Get organized.* You cannot take quality notes by sitting down in class, pulling whatever scrap of paper you have from your bag, and scribbling down what the professor says. You need to be intentional about keeping tidy notes in one place. The first decision you will need to make to keep yourself organized is whether you will take notes on paper or using a computer. Computers provide you more

---

[4] Diane Bone, *The Business of Listening* (Los Altos, CA: Crisp Publications, 1988), 5.

[5] One that we commend to you is the Cornell note-taking system. This system provides a simple methodology for taking, organizing, and reviewing notes. See http://lsc.cornell.edu/study-skills/cornell-note-taking -system/, accessed August 2, 2019.

flexibility for storage, organization, and editing but can also present you with distractions. If you record your notes on paper, you may find it easier to focus on the lecture material. Whichever method you use, make sure that you keep your notes related to a particular class in one place. Store your notes—whether in a computer file, notebook, or binder—in such a way that you can go back and review them by topic and by the date each lecture was given.

2. *List relevant material.* The key word here is *relevant.* As you are listening to the lecture, make sure you write down the major points your professor discusses. Learning to identify relevant material is a skill that takes time to learn, so you will get better at this throughout your studies. To begin with, look for material your professor lists in PowerPoint slides or writes on the board. He may even say "pay close attention to this topic" during the lecture. Once you record a relevant point, include information that demonstrates why it is important. For example, if you are taking a U.S. History course and realize "The Declaration of Independence" is a key point of the lecture, you need to write it down and note why it is important: "This document was a formal declaration of the independence of the thirteen American colonies from England." You will not be able to write down all the things your professor says. So, learning to list relevant materials is an essential skill.

3. *Review using course materials.* After the lecture is complete, you need to review your notes. You may be able to do this quickly before you leave class, or you may need to take time at the end of the day to review your notes from all of the day's courses. As you review, look at any course material the professor provided for the lecture. If the professor gave a handout or posted a PowerPoint presentation online, look at that material and compare it to your notes. Ask, "Do my notes include all of the important information from this material?" If not, make the necessary changes.

4. *Summarize your notes*. Think of this step as making a study guide as you go through the class. After you review your notes using course material, put in a summary section at the bottom of the page. Try to condense the entire lecture down to two or three major points. If you do this faithfully, then you will be able to use your summaries as the basis of your study guide when you review for tests. You will be surprised how this practice can help you remember the material and ultimately be ready for the exams.

Taking lecture notes teaches a skill that will serve you well far beyond the classroom. If you become an effective note taker, then you will have the ability to pull relevant information from large amounts of material. In professional settings, you will need to do this on a regular basis. My (Cory's) brother Jake works in industrial sales. One of the reasons that he excels at his job is his ability to use note-taking to turn conversations with project managers into partnerships with his company. Jake can hear what they say, efficiently record the relevant information, and then review his notes to find exactly how his company can meet the needs of his customers. Though he does not work in an academic setting, his ability to take notes equips him for success in his job.

Reading for Your Class

Reading for your courses can be a daunting task. Some students naturally love to read and spend much of their free time with a book in hand. Other students read only when required to do so and see reading as a chore. One thing both types of learners likely have in common is that they struggle to read when they begin their college coursework. Reading effectively during your academic work is not as simple as liking to read or not liking to read. Don't get us wrong: a love of reading and exposure to other books does help, but all students will need to develop special skills in order to read well for their courses.

In high school, most of your reading was likely done for literature classes and may have added up to only a few poems and essays each week with a longer work like a novel each year. College and graduate school reading is far more demanding. You will likely have to read, at minimum, the textbook for each of your courses. Courses in the humanities (think English, History, Psychology, Philosophy, etc.) may require you to read the textbook plus additional books and material. This reading adds up quickly, and it is understandable that many students feel overwhelmed by it. Understanding the purpose of reading for learning and developing strategies to read efficiently and effectively will help with the feeling of being overwhelmed.

Suppose you take a course on American History and discover that the class requires you to read a textbook, a biography, and several academic articles. You may think that the professor is trying to torment students by assigning so much reading. You may also question why all of this reading is necessary; after all, you probably aren't even a history major! But let us be clear: the professor did not assign the texts for the course just to torture students. Textbooks and additional readings are used in various ways, but the most common way is to reinforce and supplement the lectures. In other words, a large part of the material you will cover in the course will be covered in the reading. Professors want you to read because we want you to learn. To learn well in your courses, you must learn to read well for your courses.

The good news is that you can improve as a reader. Even better, as Albert Mohler notes, "we can train ourselves to enjoy reading."[6] If you read with a specific strategy, then you will be able to gain a tremendous amount of information from books. When you can gain information from books, then you have the ability to learn material from any field by reading on particular topics. The more you read,

---

[6] Albert Mohler, *The Conviction to Lead* (Minneapolis, MN: Bethany House, 2012), 103.

the better you will get at reading and the better your potential for enjoying reading. If you want to become a better reader, you can start by taking the following actions:

1. *Plan your reading.* Productive reading rarely happens by accident. Set aside time throughout your week to read and know what material you need to read for each course in a given week. If you were assigned a novel or book that you must write a review of before the midterm, you need to plan your reading in a way that allows you to cover a chapter or so a week. If you fail to plan your reading, you will feel overwhelmed as your deadlines approach, and you will risk making one of the greatest mistakes students can: trying to complete tests, reviews, and papers without having read the necessary material for those assignments.

2. *Create a reading environment.* Most people don't find it helpful to just pick up a book—especially books for class—and read them wherever they happen to be. Find a regular place to read that helps you minimize distractions. This may be your campus library, a coffee shop, a chair in your room, or somewhere on the grounds of your campus. Have things ready that help you focus on reading, such as a cup of coffee or a particular type of music, when you set aside time for the task. This step looks different for each reader, but creating the reading environment that is best for you will help you minimize distractions and maximize your attention to the reading material.

3. *Know what type of material you are reading.* Not all reading materials for your courses are the same, and the things you should give attention to in your reading will change based on the type of reading material. Academic articles will have one central point supported by material throughout the article. Textbooks present you with material to help you understand an entire topic. More general academic

books make an argument supported by several key points that are usually the topics of each chapter. Some courses will require you to read works of fiction, which tell a story. Once you determine the type of book you are reading, you will know what type of material to focus on.

4. *Read with purpose.* Mortimer J. Adler and Charles Van Doren, in their classic *How to Read a Book* say, "The rules for reading yourself to sleep are easier to follow than are the rules for staying awake while reading."[7] Adler's point is that unintentional reading is boring reading. Reading with a purpose, however, drives you to find out what a book or an article means. If you want to do this, you must ask questions of the book as you read. Adler gives a great list of questions to ask as you go,[8] but we think there are two questions that you should ask of any reading: "What is the author trying to say?" and "Is the author's message true?" If you ask these questions as you read, you will be able to engage with the message of the author and form your own views of the author's message.

5. *Write in your books.* We know we are telling you to break a rule you were taught as a child, but it is a dumb rule. Karen Swallow Prior urges readers to "read with a pen, pencil, or highlighter in hand, marking in the book or taking notes on paper. The idea that books should not be written in is . . . rooted in a misunderstanding of what makes a book valuable."[9] So long as a book is *your* book—meaning you did not borrow or rent it—then writing in your books

---

[7] Mortimer J. Adler and Charles Van Doren, *How to Read a Book: The Classic Guide to Intelligent Reading*, rev. ed. (New York: Simon & Schuster, 1972), 45.

[8] Adler and Van Doren, 45–47.

[9] Karen Swallow Prior, *On Reading Well: Finding the Good Life through Great Books* (Grand Rapids: Brazos Press, 2018), 17.

can be a great help to you as a reader. Underline or highlight key points; write questions on the side of the page. This allows you to review your reading and come back to material that you identified as important or to revisit areas where you had questions.

Reading well will benefit you in your academic studies. Western education is built largely upon the idea that books are central to the educational process. Students who are good readers have the ability to overcome many hurdles to their academic success—including poor professors! If you are in a course and the professor is struggling to communicate the content, strong reading skills will allow you to receive from books what your professor may not give you in class lectures. Reading will, likewise, help you in whatever career you pursue. Employers in every field value employees who can process information from emails, policy manuals, and other professional documents. Moreover, employees who are exceptional readers have the ability to continually train themselves to address new needs in their jobs.

The true value of reading well, however, is not found in your success in the classroom or in your career. God is good to give us the ability to read because it adds to the richness of our lives. Karen Swallow Prior makes this argument beautifully: "Reading well adds to our life—not in the way a tool from the hardware store adds to our life, for a tool does us no good once lost or broken, but in the way a friendship adds to our life, altering us forever."[10] The ability of reading to add to our lives is especially true for Christians who believe that God speaks to us through the Bible—through a book. For this reason, John Piper states, "Reading well is a mediator of glory."[11]

---

[10] Prior, *On Reading Well*, 18.

[11] John Piper, *A Peculiar Glory: How the Christian Scriptures Reveal Their Complete Truthfulness* (Wheaton, IL: Crossway, 2016), 272.

Studying for and Taking Tests

Before you started college, you might have been able to pass or even do well on exams without spending any time studying. However, students rarely make it through a college degree program without learning how to study. The process of mastering study can be confusing. One of the most common objections to studying for exams we hear is that students feel that when they study for a test it does not improve their scores. If you don't know how to study, or you have studied for exams in the past and found that it did not help you on your exam, know that you are not alone! Many students struggle like this. The problem is not that studying is unworthwhile or that you are a defective student. Instead, the fact that you struggle to study in a way that helps improve your test scores indicates that you need to learn more effective methods for studying.

Not only do you need to give attention to honing your study skills, but you will also benefit from learning how to take tests well. Exams can be stressful. Preparing and taking exams using effective methods helps alleviate stress. Following the steps below will help you study for and take tests in a more effective way.

1. *Make a plan.* You need to be intentional about when and how you study. The first step in your study plan requires awareness of when you will have exams. You should begin studying at least one week before an exam. Remember, you should already be reviewing your notes for class each week. But study focuses beyond reviewing the most recent lecture and looks at all the material the exam will cover. You will need to decide how much time to give yourself to study each day based on the intensity of the exam. If you start a week ahead and study one hour each day, you will study a total of seven hours for the exam. That is the equivalent of pulling an all-night study session the night before an exam, but it is far more effective and far less stressful. Note: Part of what makes this strategy successful is the way your brain

enough about learning to seek further information. You would be surprised about how a relatively minor interaction with a student outside of class can leave a positive impression with the professor.

2. *Required course materials.* The textbooks, computer programs, or other materials you will need to do your coursework will be listed on the syllabus. Some professors will list both required material, which you must have for the course, and recommended materials, which may be useful but are not essential to completing the coursework.

3. *Grading information.* If you are in a course in which the midterm is worth 50 percent of your overall grade, you need to know that on day 1, not the day of the midterm. The good news is that a course syllabus lists how your final grade in the course is calculated based on the weight of individual assignments.

4. *Lecture and reading schedule.* Course syllabi typically include a schedule of the topics covered in lecture as well as a schedule for required readings in the class. The lecture schedule helps you know how to prepare for lectures each class meeting. The reading schedule lets you know how to stay current on your reading so that you can follow lectures and course discussions as well as be ready for tests and quizzes at the appropriate time.

5. *Assignment deadlines.* To succeed in your classes, you need to know when you have assignments due and on which days your exams will be given. The syllabus will inform you of all the due dates and assignments for the class. In chapter 5, we provide some additional advice about how to transfer these due dates from your course syllabus to a calendar so that you can keep up with all of your classes at one time.

6. *Class policies.* Some professors have policies that are specific to their classes. These may cover academic items like which style guide to use for your papers, or they may be about the behavior expected of you in class.

works. The practice of setting something aside and then reviewing it at another time or on a different day increases your learning significantly.[12]

2. *Ask about the format.* Your professor will not tell you the answers to the test questions and will likely not tell you what questions will be on the exam. However, if you ask your professor the format of the exam (essay questions, multiple choice, fill in the blanks, etc.), she will likely tell you how the test is structured. Knowing the format of an exam is tremendously beneficial as you study, because it helps you think of how you need to engage the material.

3. *Review the material.* Now it is time to go back to your notes. Review what you have identified as the most important points from each section of the course. If your professor provided you with a study guide or information about the exam, begin by addressing that material. Memorize vocabulary words by making flashcards; prepare for essays by outlining answers to possible questions; work with other students in the course to quiz yourself on the material that was emphasized in the class.

4. *Sleep.* You need to sleep before an exam. This is easy advice to give but hard advice to follow. Sleeping before exams requires you to be disciplined in your earlier study so that you aren't trying to cram at the last minute. Sleeping well before exams also requires you to be satisfied that your study is sufficient and resist the urge to spend the night before an exam learning more material. Getting enough sleep is proven to improve test scores. A recent study found that students who slept an average of eight hours a night

---

[12] P. C. Brown, H. L. Roediger, and M. A. McDaniel, *Make It Stick: The Science of Successful Learning* (Cambridge, MA: Harvard University Press), 2014.

during final exams' week performed better on their exams than students who slept fewer than eight hours a night.[13]

5. *Remain calm.* When you begin your test, remain calm. Do not let yourself get stuck on a particular answer or section at the beginning of the exam. Mark questions that are giving you trouble and return to them after you answer questions to which you know the answers. Answering some of the easier questions at the beginning of an exam can give you confidence to tackle the more difficult sections. Be deliberate about the material you put on the page. If you are a slow writer, give yourself time for essay questions. If you are taking a math exam, do not forget to check your work. Before you turn the test in, review your work. Make sure you have answered all the questions and that your name is on the cover page and/or the Scantron sheet.

6. *Review your results.* Exams serve many purposes, and all of them are ultimately meant to benefit your education. Professors don't give you exams just to decide who passes and who fails. They give you exams so that you will learn. You learn through studying and through taking the exam. Your learning should continue in your review of the exam. One of the most valuable learning opportunities you will have, in fact, is reviewing exams on which you performed poorly or even failed. If you look at such an exam as an opportunity to learn how to succeed rather than as an artifact of your failure, then you create an opportunity for future success. Remember that your goal isn't really about the grade but about learning. So learn from the mistakes you made on the exam as well.

Many students graduate and celebrate no longer having to take tests. Although it is true that most jobs will not require you to

---

[13] Michael K. Scullin, "The Eight Hour Sleep Challenge during Final Exams Week," *Teaching of Psychology* 46 (1): 55–63.

take formal tests, the study and test skills you develop as a student will take you far in life. Jobs in the twenty-first century commonly require you to learn new information and skills for success. The skills that you develop for study and test taking as a student provide you with the foundation to develop skills to learn new material and apply it throughout your career.

Kingdom Academics and Kingdom Work

I (Cory) once heard a graduate, still in his cap and gown from the graduation ceremony, exclaim, "That's it! I never have to read a book again!" I hope he was not being serious; but if he was, then this young man must have missed so much in his education. Academic skills like reading really do enable you to continue to succeed far beyond your life as a student. We have seen that academic skills have applications in your vocation as well as in your life in the classroom. Students who fail to value what and how they learned in their academic work will fail to have the career opportunities they might have had. Kingdom students need to realize that even more is at stake—leaving behind the pursuit of truth at graduation limits your ability to enjoy and prosper in the life God has given you.

From the very beginning, God gave humankind a mandate to explore creation. He told Adam to name the animals, a clear indication that Adam was to be an explorer in the marvelous environment in which God had placed him. By naming the other creatures, Adam served as God's image bearer by proclaiming truth and ordering creation according to that truth. God likewise beckons us to the same work. We are to be namers of things, communicators of truth to our world.

King Jesus comes to us with a message that he brings "abundant life" to those in the kingdom (John 10:10). While every believer is given the same gift of salvation, our callings in this world are not identical. Thus, the academic skills we are discussing will not be a part of that abundant life for every member of the kingdom. Jesus calls each of us to enjoy the work and blessings of the kingdom according to the life he calls us to live. Those who were called to other areas of obedience are granted an equally abundant life as they serve Jesus. For those of us who, in obedience to Jesus, enter a season of academic learning, Jesus graciously uses the knowledge and skills we gain on the way to magnify our ability to serve others and to enjoy him!

4

Kingdom Productivity

Productivity is not an inherently good thing; it simply refers to working within an efficient structure to do excellent work. You have the capacity to be productive at bad and evil work as well as good and just work. Productivity is valuable only when applied to a worthwhile endeavor. When you are productive in good work, you have the ability to be a better kingdom servant. Glorifying God through service to Jesus's kingdom is a glorious endeavor, and our work in it should be as productive as possible.

Productivity is often equated with efficiency, and efficiency is sometimes associated with having a clinical approach to the people and activities in your life. Think about places where you regularly encounter productivity. Banks are productive places, so productive that bank tellers have largely been replaced with ATMs that efficiently take your deposit or deliver your withdrawal. Fast food restaurants are productive; you drive up to a speaker and place an order, then three minutes later your number-2 value meal is in your passenger seat. Drug stores, check-out lines, department stores—these are spaces of efficiency. Too often they are also lacking in personal connection with people. The stereotype that between spaces of high efficiency are often spaces of low personal connection may lead you to believe that productivity is detrimental to forming personal connections. If this were the case, then a focus on productivity would be counterproductive for kingdom students. However, productivity should increase our ability to serve others rather than hinder it.

Our friend Rex is a seminary professor and is known for being an excellent scholar and teacher, as well as for his unique fashion choices (he wears lots of interesting hats). More than either of these things, however, he is known for the way he ministers to students. His care for students is reflected in a variety of ways. He answers student emails quickly and thoroughly. His social media accounts are full of photos of him and his students and vignettes expressing the high esteem in which he holds his students and colleagues. He knows the names of his students—even the ones who don't always come to class—and tries to speak to them whenever he sees them on campus. He has a profound ability to sense when a student is in a time of crisis and prioritizes ministering to such students.

Many people assume that Rex's ability to serve students in so many ways comes from particular personality traits he possesses and gifts God has given him. Of course, many of the ways he serves students do come from unique aspects of his personality and giftedness; however, his service to students goes beyond his innate abilities. One of the chief reasons Rex is such an excellent servant to his students is that he is intentional about productivity. He sets aside time each workday for reading within his field of study and answering student emails. At the beginning of each semester, he spends time going over the roll for each class and memorizing students' names! His social media posts are intentionally positive because he has a policy not to share anything other than positive family, friend, and student-related content. Rex's exceptional service to his students begins with an exceptional approach to productivity.

The truth is that no person is innately as productive as possible. This means that all of us, regardless of our personalities or gifts, need to work to be productive. Peter Drucker encourages executives to understand that productivity takes work: "To be reasonably effective it is not enough for the individual to be intelligent, to work hard or to be knowledgeable. Effectiveness is something separate, something different."[1] The fact that everyone must work on productivity skills should be a challenge to those who think they are naturally productive and an encouragement to those who have always felt doomed to being disorganized and ineffective. All kingdom students must make a conscious effort to become more productive in the work God calls them to do.

Your ability to be productive in what God calls you to do will have tremendous impact on your ability to serve others. Productivity increases your ability to be an effective kingdom servant in at least three ways.

Being Productive Provides a Consistent Witness

No matter your vocation, the people with whom you work will respect your ability to accomplish your work in a productive manner. Efficiently accomplishing your work ought to flow from a vision to accomplish everything you do with excellence; it will serve as a testimony that you are doing your work for something more than earning a paycheck. The Bible provides a standard for excellence and a reason for us to be productive in our work. Paul urges the church in Colossae, "Whatever you do, in word or in deed, do everything in the name of the Lord Jesus, giving thanks to God the Father through him" (Col 3:17). This and other similar passages make clear that Christians are to be productive in the work to which we are called.[2]

Being productive should not be about personal accolades or promotions. Both of us are blessed to be in situations where we love and respect the women and men who have authority over us in the

---

[1] Peter Drucker, *The Effective Executive: The Definitive Guide to Getting the Right Things Done* (New York: Harper, 2006), ix.

[2] The Bible provides a rich theology of work. See James M. Hamilton Jr., *Work and Our Labor in the Lord: Short Studies in Biblical Theology* (Wheaton, IL: Crossway, 2017).

workplace; however, our pursuit of productivity is not for their sake, and our standard of excellence is not measured based on their expectations. We should seek to be productive in our work so that we provide a consistent witness to the God who has called us to serve.

Being productive in what we do provides an example to believers and unbelievers of the nature of our faith. To unbelievers, the productivity of their Christian colleagues should bear witness to the fact that believers are focused on glorifying God through service to others. This may serve as a way for our unbelieving colleagues to see the good news—that Jesus glorified the Father through laying down his life for us—reflected in our daily walk of life. We are not suggesting that believers do not need to share the gospel verbally as well. Instead, when we share the gospel with unbelieving coworkers, our productive, others-focused work should provide an illustration to them of the truth of the gospel. If we are working with believers—whether in the ministry of the local church, a Christian organization, or alongside Christian coworkers in a secular organization—our productive work should serve as a witness to one another that part of what sets Christian work apart is a commitment to being productive to the glory of God. When we work in such a way, our work becomes an act of worship and a reflection of the good works in which God has equipped us to walk through the grace he has given us through Jesus (Eph 2:10).

What is true in the workplace is true for your work as a student. Wherever God has opened opportunities for you to work during this season of study—whether in class, in a job, or in a volunteer position—the way in which you work is a witness to who you are and what you believe. If you are a Christian student, you need to strive to be productive in order to have a consistent witness to those around you.

Being Productive Opens the Door for More Good Work

I (Cory) often have students come sit in my office and seek my advice about whether or not to pursue a new opportunity.

Typically, when students ask me about such things, I ask them what else they are doing in their lives. Are they doing well in class? Are they sleeping a healthy amount on a regular basis? Are they regularly attending worship services at their church? Often, I find that students are struggling in most or all of the areas I discuss with them, and my advice is that they don't need to take on a new responsibility until they find a better way to manage the responsibilities they already have.

Sometimes people struggle with doing things well because they genuinely have too much on their plates. An important part of being productive is knowing your limits and not taking on too much (more on this later). However, your capacity for the amount of good work you can accomplish increases when you develop your productivity skills. Simply put, being productive allows you to do more work with a higher degree of excellence. Some of the most productive people we know have an astounding number of responsibilities, yet their productivity skills allow them to fulfill all these responsibilities with excellence.

As a student you may feel that you are overwhelmed with all the things you *have* to do, not to mention the things you would *like* to do. We have some bad news: it may get worse. As overwhelming as student life can be, life beyond higher education is often far more chaotic.[3] Don't presume that you will live out a chaotic life during the course of your education and then get relief when you graduate. As a student you have an opportunity to learn how to tame the chaos in your life by increasing your ability to be productive throughout all your areas of responsibility. Developing such

---

[3] We know this may not be the case for all students. Some of our readers may be in school *and* have a full-time job *and* have a husband or wife and children *and* have ministry commitments. Both of us held all of these responsibilities simultaneously through parts of our educational experiences. Life may get less hectic for you when you graduate, but the added responsibility of education at this time in your life makes developing your ability to be productive that much more important.

skills in productivity is essential if you are to be a servant of Jesus's kingdom. Your time in college is an excellent chance to become more productive so that you can accomplish all you have planned.

Being Productive Makes Life More Enjoyable

Productive work for the glory of God should lead us to a place of enjoyment. God modeled this for us in his productive work of creation. After creating the heavens and the earth, God rested in his creation. God's rest on the seventh day is of tremendous importance to a theology of productivity. God's creative model in Genesis 1 demonstrates that the natural conclusion of work is rest. God's rest was not born out of exhaustion or need; instead, God rested from his creative work so that he could celebrate the goodness of his work with the creatures he had made.[4] The main implication of God's rest in creation on the seventh day is explained in the first question of the Westminster Shorter Catechism: "What is the chief end of man?" The answer the catechism gives is "Man's chief end is to glorify God, and to enjoy him forever." God gives us a model for work—and existence—that encourages us to enjoy the product of our work.

We live and work in a fallen world and so, of course, our work and productivity are impacted by our fallen state. We cannot look for our work, no matter how productive, to make us complete. Only the work of Jesus can make us complete by bringing us into perfect rest with God.[5] What we can do in our fallen world is be

---

[4] See Kenneth A. Mathews, *Genesis 1–11:26*, The New American Commentary 1A (Nashville: Broadman & Holman, 1996), 179–81.

[5] The Bible makes it clear that the product of Jesus's work in the gospel brings us into perfect rest in the presence of God. This is the force of Rev 21:3–4 when John hears in his vision a voice from God's throne proclaiming the nature of the restored world: "Look, God's dwelling is with humanity, and he will live with them. They will be his peoples, and God himself will be with them and will be their God. He will wipe away

as productive in our work as possible for the sake of enjoying the good product of our work that God gives us through his grace. Productivity in God's plan is not simply intended to help us accomplish more work, but allows us to serve him faithfully and enjoy the good gifts he gives. Often we never come to the point of enjoying the good things our labor has produced because we either never finish what we are working on, or we never take time to enjoy it. Becoming more productive in our work can increase our enjoyment of the product of our work and the process of working itself.

One of the best illustrations for how productivity makes work more enjoyable comes from considering your work as a student. If you are constantly working in chaos—pulling all-nighters, turning things in at the last minute, barely completing assignments, etc.— then you are almost certainly not enjoying the process or product of your work. When you finally finish your assignments, you are exhausted and have to crash afterward to cope. Crashing means that for several days you likely don't touch your schoolwork, so by the time you begin again, you are already behind on your upcoming assignment. And so, this process repeats, and your life remains in a state of chaos.

If this is a good description of your life as a student, we have some bad news. Things will likely not get less chaotic after you finish your academic work. We have both worked with individuals who keep a similar chaotic pace in their vocational lives. The good news is that if you work to develop skills to become more productive in your work, you can break out of a chaotic cycle. Working in a structured, productive system helps you enjoy the work you do and gives you time for structured rest in which you can enjoy and celebrate the product of your work or learning. Consider again the example of a student, but this time a productive student. Productive students are aware of upcoming deadlines and structure their lives

---

every tear from their eyes. Death will be no more; grief, crying, and pain will be no more, because the previous things have passed away."

accordingly. They have a regular routine, which gives them time in which to do their assignments. They are aware of how many commitments they can take on without overloading themselves. They are able to do their work with excellence and have time to enjoy a job well done. They take appropriate time for healthy, celebratory rest when they finish their work and are ready to start their next tasks refreshed.

What is true for you as a student will likely be true throughout your life. If you work productively, you will have greater enjoyment of your work and the results of your labor. Our challenge to kingdom students is this: begin working on your productivity skills now so that you can enjoy the life and work that God has given you.

5

A Strategy for Kingdom Productivity

Understanding the definition of productivity is necessary in order to form a strategy for developing kingdom productivity. When you hear the word "productivity," your mind likely focuses on scheduling events and appointments, getting up early, and accomplishing tasks in the most efficient way possible. These activities may be part of being productive, but they are not all that is involved. Kingdom students must understand productivity as something more than a set of practices that make them efficient people. A kingdom view of productivity must focus on the mission of being a kingdom servant. *As a kingdom student, you must develop a system of productivity that structures the actions God calls you to take within the time God calls you to take them.* To be productive based on this definition, you must develop a strategy for productivity. Kingdom productivity requires knowing your mission, setting your routine, and structuring your work.

Know Your Mission

Both of us are blessed to be alumni of New Orleans Baptist Theological Seminary. The mission statement of NOBTS is to "prepare servants to walk with Christ, proclaim His truth, and fulfill His mission." Understanding the mission statement of NOBTS is essential for understanding the work of the school. The NOBTS curriculum is set based on the mission statement; faculty members are assessed based on how their teaching fulfills the mission statement; the trustees of the seminary hold its leaders accountable to work toward the mission statement. To be a productive institution, NOBTS must measure all of her work based on her mission.

Just as institutions must understand their missions, you must also understand your mission if you are to be a productive individual. While you can formulate one overarching mission statement for all of the work you are called to do, such a broad definition is not helpful for increased productivity. Instead, work on knowing the mission for each type of work God has called you to accomplish.

Tim Challies recommends identifying all of the areas of responsibility God has given you. In Challies's system, you list all of the areas in which God has called you to work and then develop a mission statement for each area.[1] If you use this method for determining your mission, you ensure that you understand each area of your life and work as an outlet for loving God through working toward the mission of the kingdom. Determining a specific mission for each area of your life will force you to think about the various responsibilities you have and the tasks that come from them.

As a student, you have various areas of responsibility, and you need to understand how God is calling you to work in each one. Your areas of responsibility will include your coursework, your ministry and volunteer work, and your work with student organizations. You will also have areas of responsibility stemming

---

[1] Tim Challies, *Do More Better: A Practical Guide to Productivity* (Minneapolis, MN: Cruciform Press, 2015), 27–43.

from family. Your family responsibilities will change significantly based on your situation in life. They could include parenting, your marriage, or maintaining your relationship with your parents, siblings, and extended family. On top of these areas, you also need to remember personal care. If you are not taking care of yourself physically and mentally, you are not being an effective servant of Jesus's kingdom.

We recommend listing all the areas of responsibility in your life and developing a mission statement for each of them. These mission statements become essential for knowing what sort of work you should be doing and what types of tasks should be associated with that work.

Select Your Work

As a student you have many opportunities to volunteer for roles of service and leadership. Many of these positions are great opportunities to gain experience for your career to build your résumé. If you are asked to serve in a leadership position, you should accept this opportunity if it fits within your calling and passion; but one mark of a mature, productive student is not always saying yes to these opportunities. Students who instantly say yes to every opportunity often become loaded down with so much to do that they can't do anything well. Unfortunately, these are often some of the most gifted students (thus the reason they were asked to do so much), but they find themselves incapable of using the gifts God has given them for excellent work because they have too much to do.

Not saying yes to every opportunity may seem like a bad idea—especially if you are just starting your academic work. You want to gain experience, do ministry, and be a part of your community, so jumping at every opportunity to serve seems natural. What you must realize is that if you say yes to every opportunity that comes your way, you will eventually have more work than you can handle. When you take on too much work, you reach a point where you cannot be productive regardless of your routines or structure.

There is more good work to do in the world than you can do yourself. Do not be surprised or disappointed by this. You are a human being. Admitting that you are limited in the good work you can accomplish is a proclamation that you are not the redeemer of the world but someone who has been invited to participate in the work of Jesus, the Messiah who redeems all things.

Your inability to accomplish all of the good work that needs to be done in the world around you should cause you to rejoice in God's grace. No one is doing the good work of the gospel alone! Paul gives a beautiful explanation of the diversity of gifts God gives to Christians in 1 Corinthians 12. Paul uses the image of one body with many members, each with a particular role to fill. We are not to try to do all of the work of the church, only to use the gifts God has given us to do the work he calls us to do. Paul makes this clear when he says, "A manifestation of the Spirit is given to each person for the common good" (1 Cor 12:7). God has given you particular gifts for a particular work that will, by God's grace, play a part in the much larger work of the kingdom.

Randy Alcorn argues, "The key to a productive and content life is 'planned neglect'—knowing what NOT to do, and being content with saying no to truly good, sometimes fantastic, opportunities."[2] Alcorn's strategy of "planned neglect" is a helpful way for all of us to think about many of the opportunities that come our way. When we are presented with an opportunity for good work, our default answer should not be "Yes, I will do that!" Instead, we should consider the opportunity and assess whether or not it fits within one of our areas of responsibility and within our mission for that area of responsibility.

I (Norris) have often struggled saying no to new opportunities of service. I thought that if it's a godly activity I should say yes.

---

[2] Randy Alcorn, "A Lesson Hard Learned: Being Content with Saying No to Truly Good Opportunities," Eternal Perspectives Ministries, November 10, 2014, https://www.epm.org/blog/2014/Nov/10/saying-no.

Several years ago, I heard a conference speaker stress that every "yes" entails a "no" to something else. For example, a "yes" to a preaching invitation that involves travel means a "no" to spending time with my family on those dates. I still travel and speak, but each opportunity is filtered through this principle that every "yes" equals a "no."

Set Your Routine

Once you have selected which work you need to accomplish, you can start focusing on the best way to do it. One of the best methods to accomplish your work with consistent excellence is to create a routine. Routines help us order our work within our busy lives.

In my (Cory's) house, I have a small workshop in the basement. In the workshop is a table that I use for projects. On the table and on the wall above it, I have various tools organized in readiness for working on a project. When working in my shop, I automatically know where the necessary tools are located and can access them easily. Organizing the tools on my work table does not make the work I do there easier, but my work in the space is more productive and efficient because I don't waste time looking for the right tool. Working from a routine has a similar effect on our daily output.

A routine can do for time what organization of a work area does for space. Just as physical organization addresses the question "where are the necessary things for my work?" a routine answers the question "when is the necessary time for my work?" Routines orient the daily rhythms of your life toward the good work you are called to do.

A routine should orient both your committed time (time you are committed to being in class, at an appointment, at church, etc.) and your non-committed time. If you want to maximize your productivity, you must not be content with a routine that deals only with your committed time. Being where you need to be when you have committed to being there is essential, but your non-committed time is often some of the most important time for accomplishing your mission. Non-committed time is when you do homework, prepare for a presentation, and research to answer a friend's question about the Bible. You must set aside some non-committed time for rest and sleep, two things that are essential if you are to be a productive servant of the kingdom of God.[3]

The work that takes place in non-committed time requires self-motivation. Our experience is that most students reach college and grad school with adequate skill in doing work performed under supervision. High school tends to make you an expert at performing work while an authority figure is in the room ensuring that you do what you must to succeed. Success in higher education requires you to learn how to do work in and out of class. Your studies will require you to go beyond typical homework and participate in serious research and learning outside of the classroom. In addition to these new educational responsibilities, you must consider how your other avenues of service will require self-motivated work.

People have different perspectives on how to formulate daily routines. Matt Perman recommends making a schedule that accounts for each hour of your week.[4] Constructing such a detailed schedule may not be an ideal project for everyone; but if you don't know where to start on a routine, this is a great way to begin visualizing how to structure your time. I (Norris) would cringe at a schedule this structured, but tracking time like this might be helpful for seeing how you are spending your time and how you may need to change your routine to be more productive.

Another way to structure your work is to allocate your daily tasks within larger chunks of time. You can do this by breaking each day of the week up into mornings, afternoons, and evenings. Identify what units of this time are already devoted to commitments—attending class lectures, serving at church, practice

---

[3] See Kevin DeYoung, *Crazy Busy: A (Mercifully) Short Book about a (Really) Big Problem* (Wheaton, IL: Crossway, 2013), 89–99.

[4] Matt Perman, *What's Best Next: How the Gospel Transforms the Way You Get Things Done* (Grand Rapids: Zondervan, 2014), 196–205.

for an athletic team, etc. The chunks of time in your week when you do not have any commitments present you with opportunities to be intentional about accomplishing the work you have selected to accomplish the mission God has given you.

One of the greatest challenges to setting a routine as a student can be the ever-changing nature of your weekly and even daily schedule. Regular changes in the number of school assignments, work schedules, and time spent with friends can make getting into a pattern difficult. One way to alleviate this difficulty is to stick to at least a very basic routine whenever possible. If your friends ask you to go out for lunch during your regular study time, seriously consider whether or not you should interrupt your schedule. Sometimes breaking your routine is unavoidable. But when your routine is interrupted, work hard to get back to structure as soon as possible.

However you form your routine, the goal should be that you have an idea of *when* you should be doing *what* activity. Keep in mind that routines should give you a framework for accomplishing quality work as well as participating in quality rest. If you enjoy streaming Netflix, playing video games, playing pickup basketball, or reading Harry Potter, that is fine. Just know when and for how long you can responsibly participate in these leisure activities. When you work and rest within the framework of a routine, you eliminate the stress of wondering if you are doing the right thing and are free to focus on the activity at hand.

Structure Your Work

Once you have a routine established, it is time to structure your work. A routine lets you know *when* to do work; now you must determine *what* work to do in a given day. The best way to structure your work is to use two basic tools: a calendar and a to-do list. These may seem too obvious; but we assure you, they are powerful and will help you be successful at whatever you are called to do.

Calendars give you the ability to know what events are on your horizon and how those events should affect your daily work. To-do lists provide you with categorized tasks you intend to accomplish in a given day. When used in tandem, these tools help you ensure that you are prepared and present for the work God has called you to do.

Before we get into the specifics of how to use calendars and to-do lists effectively, let's answer a common objection to using these tools. We often hear people say, "I don't like to confine myself to a calendar or list! I take life one moment at a time and that works for me!" Taking life one moment at a time may work for you, but we would be willing to bet that it does not always work for the people you are serving or the people with whom you are serving.

One of us once led a group on a mission trip that required significant physical labor. With the strenuous nature of the work in mind, those coming on the trip were asked to meet to depart for the trip early in the morning so we could reach our destination in time to get a good night's sleep. All of the people going on the trip arrived on time but one. Our departure was delayed for hours because of one person who had forgotten we were leaving that particular morning. When the individual arrived, we were told, "I like to fly by the seat of my pants." Of course, the problem is that the rest of the group suffered because we had sacrificed sleep to be where we needed to be on time. The group arrived late to our destination and worked our first day on just a few hours of sleep because one individual was not the sort of person who liked to "confine" life by planning ahead. We tell you this story to illustrate an important point: failing to be organized because you think that is part of your personality is selfish. Using tools to structure your work is not about confining yourself; it is about becoming a better servant to others.

Using a Calendar

Each semester of your academic career, you will walk into class the first day and review the syllabus. The syllabus contains a significant amount of vital information, such as which textbooks you should buy, what content will be covered in the course, and when your professor keeps office hours. The syllabus also gives you your assignments for the course and the day on which they are due. Syllabus information is usually organized neatly on the page, and you may be tempted to think that such a well-organized document is all you need to keep yourself organized throughout the semester. And you are right—if taking that one class is all you have to do for the entire semester! Full-time undergraduate students typically take four or five courses per semester (many more in some majors); full-time graduate students typically take three or four courses each semester. You cannot keep up with all of the assignments for all of your courses just by referencing your various syllabi throughout the semester. On top of your academic work, you also have extracurricular activities, meetings with friends, church responsibilities, and commitments to stay in contact with your family (don't forget to call your mom!). How can you be all the places you need to be and prepared to do all the things you need to do?

You need a calendar! A calendar is simply a tool that allows you to keep up with all of your appointments and commitments. What a syllabus does for an individual course, a calendar does for all of your activities. When you use a calendar, you liberate yourself from having to remember times and dates from various syllabi, text messages, emails, and conversations by bringing all of that information into one place where you can easily view it. Also, a calendar gives you an opportunity to plan ahead. When using a calendar, you are able not only to note that the paper is due the last week of class, but also to place a reminder or series of reminders to yourself a few weeks before that to work on the assignment. Thus, you won't arrive at the end of the semester and be surprised by what is due.

When choosing what calendar you use, you have a wide variety of options. A quick walk through a bookstore or department store—especially near the beginning of the year—demonstrates that options abound for paper calendars. Some people prefer using these, but we would suggest you use a digital calendar. Several easy-to-use digital calendars are available for free. If you have an email account through a service like Apple Mail, Outlook, or Google, then you have a digital calendar available as a part of that account. There are two major benefits to using a digital calendar:

1. You can always access your calendar through an app on your smartphone. Rather than having to keep a paper calendar with you throughout the day, you can check your calendar simply by tapping an icon on your phone.

2. You can integrate alerts through email, texts, and phone that help you be where you need to be when you need to be there.

We recommend using the digital calendar that is associated with your email address if possible. If you have a student email, it likely gives you this option. Once you have selected a digital calendar, stick with it. If you start recording events on multiple calendars, you will not be able to keep up with all you have to do.

Once you have selected a calendar, there are three steps you need to go through to use it effectively:

1. *Determine which types of events you need to record on your calendar.* Tasks such as brushing your teeth or taking out the trash in your room are (hopefully!) not things about which you need to be reminded by your calendar. Classes or other regular weekly activities may or may not need to be noted. Some people like to include them to help them see a breakdown of their week; others may not find recording these meetings helpful. The items that definitely belong on your calendar are deadlines, meetings, and events that do not occur on a regular basis. If you schedule a meeting with a professor, have a paper due, or commit to switch shifts with a coworker, these items must go on your calendar.

2. *When you make a commitment, enter it into your calendar.* Jesus commands us to be the sort of people who take things seriously when we make a commitment. He tells us "let your 'yes' mean 'yes,' and your 'no' mean 'no'" (Matt 5:37). When you tell someone you will be present and

prepared for something, you have made a commitment. If your "yes" is to mean "yes," then you need to make sure you remember what you have committed to do and when you have committed to do it. To ensure that, enter your commitments into your calendar immediately.

3. *Review your calendar on a regular basis.* Getting information onto your calendar is not enough; now you have to do something with it. If you don't remember to review your calendar regularly, then the information you record will not do you any good. We recommend doing a quick check of your calendar each morning. Review your commitments for the day in detail so you will know when you need to be at specific appointments. Do a quick check of appointments and deadlines for the entire week. Do you have a paper deadline in five days? Chances are that needs to affect what you do today. Once a week, make sure you look at the entire month and note which major projects are on the horizon. By the way, the daily check-ins are great opportunities to pray for the hours ahead and ask the Lord to guide you.

Creating a To-Do List

To-do lists are not as essential as calendars, but they are helpful tools. A calendar keeps track of your appointments and deadlines that are a part of your work; a to-do list keeps track of the tasks that you need to complete to accomplish your work. To-do lists also allow you to prioritize your work throughout the day so that you can ensure you make the most necessary tasks a priority.

As with calendars, there are digital applications that allow you to create to-do lists.[5] Although using an app for a to-do list is

---

[5] Some of the more popular to-do-list apps are Apple Reminders, Todoist, Google Keep, Evernote, and Wunderlist.

helpful, we do not find it as necessary as keeping a digital calendar. Some people, in fact, find it most helpful to carry a small notebook or to keep their to-do list on their desk or countertop.

To-do lists provide you with the ability to organize tasks that need to be done in a given day or tasks that need to be done for a particular project. You may, for instance, want to list out all of the tasks you need to accomplish for a day (do math homework, meet Austin for coffee, submit paperwork to financial aid), or you may want to list out all the tasks you need to do to complete the presentation for your English class (read book, create PowerPoint, design handout). Using to-do lists allows you to progress through given tasks for the day and can help you prioritize tasks. If I continue to see "turn in paperwork for scholarship" on my to-do list, I am more likely to prioritize that important task than if I do not write it down and get caught up doing other work instead.

If you choose to use a to-do list, do it well. Following these three steps will help you maximize the effectiveness of your to-do list:

1. *Keep your to-do list in a consistent place.* This could be an app on your phone or a notebook you keep in your pocket, purse, or backpack. Even scrap paper works as long as you keep it on a countertop, stuck to the refrigerator, or on your desk. If you keep lists in different places, they will never prove very useful because you will not be able to refer to a list without wasting time looking for it.

2. *Organize your to-do list by prioritizing the tasks you need to accomplish.* Ideally, you would always be able to accomplish all of your tasks in a given day. In reality, this will not always happen. That's why you need to make sure that you note the most important tasks on your list. You can do this by either listing essential tasks first or by writing them in bold or putting a star beside them. These tasks may not always need to be done first, though. Often eliminating a few tasks that can be accomplished in two to five minutes is emotionally helpful. Your essential tasks need to be

noted on your list, however, so you can see what *must* be done by the end of the day.

3. *Move items you do not accomplish onto the to-do list for the next day.* We recommend scrapping your to-do list at the end of every day. If you have any items left over, move them to your next list. Sometimes you will notice tasks that keep bouncing from list to list. When you do, you need to decide whether that task needs to be removed from your list entirely for a while (if you haven't done it yet, is it really that important?) or if the task needs to be moved to priority status on your next day's list.

Give Yourself a Break

We believe that knowing your mission, selecting your work, setting your routine, and structuring your work will make you a better student and will equip you to be a better servant to God's kingdom. We also want to caution you against being too rigorous as you apply this method. The system we have laid out is meant to help you do what God is calling you to do, but it is not the calling itself. Sometimes you will say yes to opportunities you should have turned down, fall out of routine, and forget to add appointments to your calendar. When that happens, don't beat yourself up; learn from it. Learning, after all, is what students are supposed to do. Remember that over time you will get better at the process of being productive. As you do, you will become an increasingly better student and an increasingly more effective servant in the kingdom of God.

Kingdom Leadership

If you wish to be effective in your academic career and in your service to Jesus's kingdom, then you must be an effective leader. Leadership is a necessity whether or not you ever hold the top position within an organization. If you work with a group of people to accomplish a task, then you are involved in leadership.

Some people think about leadership as a function of certain personality types. Consider two different types of students and their abilities as leaders. Student number 1 is outspoken, often proclaiming her opinions to her professors and classmates. She is quick to make a decision and enjoys communicating her decisions to others. Student number 2 is quiet; she is rarely the first person to speak when someone asks a question. She gradually comes to decisions and does not always feel that sharing her decision is needed. Which of these students is the best leader?

The answer is that we do not have enough information to tell. Some people are outspoken and opinionated and use these traits to be great leaders. Many world leaders, CEOs, and entrepreneurs have this kind of personality. However, these same traits, when applied in the wrong way, can become detrimental to your ability to lead. The same holds true for more quiet and reserved individuals.

Such people have a unique potential to lead in a thoughtful and intentional way, though they may have to be more intentional in situations that demand swift and decisive action.[1] Personality traits help and hinder leaders in various ways, but your effectiveness is not based on your personality type.

We share this with you so that you will know that everyone has potential as a leader. You may think that you are not the sort of person who is gifted with leadership potential, but the truth is that you have and will continue to have unique opportunities to lead in various ways. In any career where you will be working with groups of people to accomplish a task, you will need to have strong leadership skills. In your academic work, in your career, and in your service to Jesus's kingdom, you will have the opportunity to influence others. Growing as a leader equips you to influence others in a way that glorifies God.

Defining Leadership

Defining "leadership" is difficult. More than twenty years ago, Burt Nanus identified more than 850 definitions of leadership.[2] The definitions of leadership have only grown in number since that time. Looking at various definitions can be helpful, but we want you to focus on a simple explanation of leadership that equips you to lead in any situation in which you are working with multiple people. Our definition for leadership is *equipping those around you to do good work.*

I (Cory) stumbled on this definition of leadership when dialoguing with my two best and most important students—my two

---

[1] For a look at how those with a more introverted personality have much to offer in the tasks of communication and leadership, see Susan Cain, *Quiet: The Power of Introverts in a World That Can't Stop Talking* (New York: Broadway Books, 2012).

[2] Warren Bennis and Burt Nanus, *Leaders: Strategies for Taking Charge* (New York: HarperCollins, 1997), 4.

daughters. My girls are at ages at which getting them to pick up their toys is a constant challenge. Recently they had a friend over to play, and cleaning up the mess at the end of the day became a huge ordeal. Rather than pick up the toys, which the three girls were told to do repeatedly, they instead dumped all the toys in the room into one big pile. Actually, only my three-year-old dumped the toys. My five-year-old and the friend stood by and laughed and cheered her on.

My breakthrough on defining leadership came when I was discussing with my five-year-old why I was disappointed in her actions. She had not been actively disobeying her parents in the dumping matter, but she was actively encouraging her sister by cheering her on in doing the wrong thing. I told her that I expected her to be a leader. She asked me, "How do I do that?" My answer to her surprised me and has changed the way I think of leadership: "You lead by helping those around you do what is right." In other words, I encouraged her to equip her sister and friend to do good work.

The Leadership Spectrum

Most definitions understand the position of a leader as being someone at the top of a leadership structure. Peter Drucker defines a leader as "someone with followers." He goes on to say that "without followers there can be no leaders."[3] Drucker's definition is a good one, but we need to realize that we may not always have followers in a formal sense. Everyone who works with a group of people, however, has the ability to equip those around them to do good work.

Leadership occurs on a spectrum. We are often tempted to think that situations are clearly defined in a leader/follower dynamic, but this is rarely the case. Consider what happens when you walk into a classroom. You may be tempted to think that the professor is the leader and the students are the followers, as if the

---

[3] Peter F. Drucker, "Your Leadership Is Unique," *Christianity Today Pastors*, July 11, 2007, https://www.christianitytoday.com/pastors/2007/july-online-only/le-614-614054.html.

entire leadership relationship can be defined by these categories. However, classroom leadership is not that simple. The professor in a classroom is teaching that course because the president and trustees set a vision for the school. The provost and deans constructed a curriculum to match that vision, and the department chair scheduled the professor to teach that particular course. The professor enters the classroom further down the chain of leadership than you might expect.

In the same way, students in the classroom are not just followers, but many are also functioning as leaders there. Ask any professor if all sections of a class are the same even if the subject, classroom, and textbook are identical. They will tell you sections are not the same because the students are different. All classrooms have student leaders. In good classes, these leaders are students who set an example by showing an interest in the class material and being respectful toward peers. Classes in which student leaders show a lack of interest in the subject matter and/or belittle their professor and classmates are often miserable for professor and students alike.

The example of the classroom illustrates that leadership is not as simple as identifying leaders and their followers. Leadership occurs on a spectrum; all of us are followers in some sense and leaders in another. We have to keep the context of leadership in mind when we define what it means to be a leader.

Understanding leadership as occurring on a spectrum is vital for kingdom students. Remembering that you have a role to play in the various groups to which you belong is essential to succeeding as you serve God in your academic work, your career, and your gospel-centered service to Jesus. We have identified specific reasons leadership ought to matter for kingdom students.

Doing Good Work Requires Communicating a Mission for That Good Work

All vocations involve working together with others. Try to think of a job in which a person works only on his own, never interacting with others. Such jobs do not exist. All work is done, at some level, with and for others. Many teachers and professors joke that "teaching would be easy if it weren't for the students!" This joke may not actually be funny, but it does illustrate an important truth: teaching without students would be ridiculous because teaching is all about students. Students could just as easily say that "learning would be so easy if it weren't for the professors," but this would present the same problem. Professors are essential for learning in a formal setting—at least we hope they are, because that's how we pay the bills!

Whatever job you do, you will need to work together with other people as you do it. One of the most essential skills you can develop, therefore, is the ability to make others better at what they are called to do. In his book *The Fred Factor*, Mark Sanborn says that the most important job skill in the twenty-first century is "the ability to create value for customers without spending money to do it."[4] While Sanborn's advice is geared toward customer service, the same skill is just as vital for leadership. Whatever work you are participating in, you can find ways to equip others to do good work without spending a dime in the process.

As a student, you are constantly learning information that equips you to do well in a wide range of activities and vocations. If you also commit to developing leadership skills during your studies, then you will be able to go beyond bringing your own skills to the work and ministry before you. If you are a capable leader, then you will be able to equip others in your business, church, school, or other organization to do better work themselves.

An essential area of leadership is communicating the mission a group of people has for accomplishing their work. We have already discussed how essential it is to know your mission for individual productivity. If a group of people are to be productive, then they

---

[4] Mark Sanborn, *The Fred Factor: How Passion in Your Work and Life Can Turn the Ordinary into the Extraordinary* (Colorado Springs, CO: Waterbrook, 2004), 12.

must be united in a common mission. Great leaders at the top of organizations are able to communicate the mission of their institutions or businesses to all of their employees. Chick-fil-A is famous for providing exceptional customer service. One of the reasons that it has excelled in this area is that Truett Cathy, the company's founder, instilled into each member of his team a vision for excellence in customer service. He made it clear that considering serving others a pleasure is part of the mission of his company.

Communicating vision is not always the product of top-down leadership. Some of the best leaders we know are people who are not in roles at the top of an organization's leadership structure. My (Cory's) job at the hardware store in high school helped me learn how all people in an organization can communicate the mission of an organization. The store was known for being the sort of place where people were friendly and helpful, no matter how small the problem. One of the most vital leaders in communicating the mission of the store to all the employees was a man named Mr. Herb. Mr. Herb was not a manager; he was a retiree who worked part time at the store to have something productive to do with his spare time. As a young man, I found it was not just the store owner or my supervisor who equipped me to fit the culture of the store—it was Mr. Herb. When a customer came in looking for an obscure plumbing fitting or needing help fixing an old lamp, Mr. Herb would call me over and patiently teach me how to help the customer. Mr. Herb equipped me to do good work by telling me and showing me how to fulfill the mission put before us at the store.

Whatever your role in a group of people, you will have an opportunity to equip others to do their work better by telling them and showing them the mission they are working to accomplish. Whether you are working in a classroom or a boardroom, a hospital or a restaurant, the ability to communicate the vision of the institution will be one of the greatest skills you can possess. As a student, you need to learn how to lead people by communicating the mission of good work to others.

Christian Community Requires Leadership

All of creation bears witness to the fact that humans were not designed to live their lives alone. The Bible makes this clear when God observes Adam alone in the garden of Eden and proclaims, "It is not good for the man to be alone" (Gen 2:18). We were created to interact with our fellow humans in the good world that God has given us. When you consider the world around you, the communal nature of life is apparent. Lonely people are rarely (if ever) happy people. Most *want* to be in fellowship with one another.

If Christians are to join together in communities, they will need leaders. Remember that leadership is not just something that comes from one or two people. Leadership is necessary in Christian community because every Christian has a vested interest in helping equip those around them to do good work. The book of Hebrews reminds us of our leadership obligation to one another: "And let us watch out for one another to provoke love and good works, not neglecting to gather together, as some are in the habit of doing, but encouraging each other, and all the more as you see the day approaching" (Heb 10:24–25).

If we are to function together in Christian community, then we must all take part in leading one another toward the work and worship God intends for us. Kingdom students must develop their skills as leaders so that they can function within the Christian community in such a way that they equip others in their sphere of influence to do good work.

Christian Evangelism Requires Leadership

Leadership skills are necessary not only for interaction with other believers, but also help us fulfill God's command to influence those outside the people of God. The Bible is clear in both the Old and New Testaments that God's people are to be his representatives to those who do not worship him. In the Old Testament, God makes a covenant specifically with Abraham and his descendants. The purpose of God's relationship with Abraham is not, however, only for Abraham and his children. From the very first description of God's covenant with Abraham and his family, God makes it clear that he intends for them to be a blessing to all the families of the earth (Gen 12:3). The New Testament commands Christians, part of Abraham's offspring by faith in Christ, to reach out to those who do not know God through Jesus Christ with the good news that Jesus has made a way for all people to join the family of God. Carrying this message of good news to others is mandated in Matt 28:19–20 where Jesus commands all his disciples, "Go, therefore, and make disciples of all nations, baptizing them in the name of the Father and of the Son and of the Holy Spirit, teaching them to observe everything I have commanded you. And remember, I am with you always, to the end of the age."

God desires his people to actively seek out those who are outside the faith family and beckon them to join the people of God through trusting in Jesus Christ. Not only that, but the Bible makes clear that individual Christians have a role to play in the discipleship of those who come into the Christian faith. The fact that all Christians are called to *lead* nonbelievers into the faith and *lead* other believers to grow in their faith indicates how vital leadership skills are in the life of all believers.

Leadership is not just important for career success. Kingdom students should recognize that developing as a leader equips you to be faithful to the commands of Scripture to evangelize and disciple those around you. You won't find this aspect of leadership emphasized in books or courses geared toward corporate executives or political movers and shakers. However, as a student who sets the advancement of Jesus's kingdom as your highest goal, learning to lead for the sake of evangelism and discipleship is the most important work to which you can apply yourself.

Your time in higher education provides you with a unique opportunity to hone leadership skills. You are surrounded by people you can equip to do good work. Think back to our illustration about how leadership occurs on a spectrum in the classroom.

Consider the fact that every time you step into one of your classes you have an opportunity to equip your classmates to do good work, often by the very example you set as a student in the course. Your time in college or graduate school also means that you are likely surrounded by capable leaders from whom you can learn. If you identify these women and men and seek to intentionally learn from their leadership styles, you will have an opportunity to grow as a leader yourself.

7

A Strategy for Kingdom Leadership

Before we lay out a specific strategy for developing leadership skills, consider what you are attempting to accomplish in your educational pursuits. Education requires both learning and doing. As you are studying in your degree program, you are preparing yourself to enter a particular field, and to that end you are beginning to put the skills you are learning into practice. Philosophy students may spend a significant amount of time gaining information about their field, but eventually they must do the work of a philosopher by sharing their thoughts and analysis of critical issues. Chemistry students spend a significant amount of time learning from a textbook about chemical reactions. Eventually, they must be willing to take out a beaker and perform their own experiments to master their discipline. A strategy for developing as a leader will likewise involve both gaining information and putting that information into practice as you do the work of a leader.

Identify Areas in Which You Have Influence

John Maxwell makes the bold claim that "leadership is influence—nothing more, nothing less."[1] Our definition of leadership understands that there is a good deal more to leading than influence, but we do believe that you cannot lead if you don't have influence among others. To begin honing your leadership skills as a student, you need to identify areas in which you have—or could potentially have—influence. Seeking areas in which you can be influential, however, is not the same as seeking to be viewed as an influential person among your peers. Remember that we are called to imitate Jesus, who understood leadership as service. He reminded his disciples that the mission of his earthly ministry was not to be served but to serve (Matt 20:28). Seek areas in which you can influence others to do good work, not areas in which you can influence others in order to elevate yourself.

Think of how you can influence your classmates and professor in each of your classes in a way that equips them to do better work. Do you have a class in which your classmates often behave in a manner that is distracting to the students and the professor? Consider how you can intentionally behave in a manner that helps offset their behavior. Do you have classmates who seem frustrated in their inability to understand the material in the course? Offer to study with them or, if you are not particularly strong in that course, introduce them to a student who is thriving in the course so that they can receive the assistance they need. Do you have a professor who gives no opportunity for student participation in the class? Read on upcoming lecture topics and find an opportunity to ask questions that probe more deeply into the material. If your professor realizes students are interested in the lecture topic, he may be more engaged with students in the future. Perhaps you can see an application of the material to your daily life. Do not

---

[1] John Maxwell, *The 21 Irrefutable Laws of Leadership: Follow Them and People Will Follow You* (Nashville: Thomas Nelson, 1998), 18.

hesitate to identify the application and ask for clarification. By doing so, you may be leading the whole class to apply the material appropriately.

Another area where you may have the ability to influence others is in student organizations around campus. I (Cory) am blessed to work with students in our Baptist Collegiate Ministry (BCM) at Shorter University. One of the reasons that I enjoy working with this group so much is that they have a tremendous amount of influence over our campus. Students involved with BCM are equipping the student body to do good work and reaching students with the gospel of Jesus in more ways than I can as a professor in the classroom. Students who participate in BCM exercise the opportunity to lead their fellow classmates by having influence within the student organization.

Christian ministry groups do not provide the only leadership opportunities on campus. Greek life, athletics, intramurals, residence life, and many other groups are excellent areas in which to exercise the kind of influence that allows you to equip others to do good work. When you look for groups in which you can participate, make sure that you select groups that have good work at the heart of their mission. If you join a group that exists primarily to party or to create an elitist environment for the senior members of the group, then that will not be a good venue in which to exercise your influence around others in a positive, God-honoring manner.

Your opportunities to exercise influence are not limited to your campus. In fact, the primary area for you to get involved in leadership is your local church. Keep in mind that as a Christian, your primary arena for service is the church. The same holds true for your leadership. Since we are defining leadership as equipping others to do good work, then leadership is itself a labor of service to others. A common student objection to getting involved in church is, "I don't have enough time." True, pursuing your degree is time-consuming work, but it is no excuse for not getting involved in a local church. People far busier than you have served and are serving to lead others in local churches.

On January 20, 1977, Jimmy Carter took the oath of office as the president of the United States. On Sunday, January 23, he went to First Baptist Church in Washington, DC, and, after being asked, volunteered to help teach Sunday school. Carter's faithfulness to attend and lead in a local church while holding one of the most difficult and time-consuming jobs in the world is a challenge to all of us. No matter how busy your schedule is, make time to get involved in worship and leadership in your local church. Work in an area in which you are gifted and help equip fellow believers to grow in their faith and proclaim the gospel to the nations.

Identify Your Role on the Leadership Spectrum

As you identify areas in which you have influence, you also need to identify the appropriate way to exercise your influence in those particular areas. Regardless of the skills or passion you can bring to a group of people, your ability to equip them to do good work will be limited if you don't identify your role within the group. Illustrations of would-be leaders who don't understand their role on the leadership spectrum are plentiful.

I (Cory) once had a coworker who desperately wanted to be a leader. This person was bright, driven, and had excellent communication skills as well as everything needed to equip others to do good work. What prevented this person from being an effective leader was that much of her communication with coworkers revolved around pointing out minor infractions of company policies. Rather than taking newer employees under her wing to demonstrate how good work ought to be done, she criticized those around her for failing to follow the rules. This gifted employee tried to fill the role of a supervisor rather than a coworker. Because she failed to understand her role on the leadership spectrum, she tended to have a negative influence on her coworkers.

The consequences of misidentifying your role on the leadership spectrum are even more consequential if you have more authority within a group of people. Both of us work with and care deeply about churches. One of the problems we often see in church life is pastors failing to understand their role in the leadership spectrum. Sometimes this comes from a pastor attempting to dominate those he leads. Rather than taking the role of a servant leader, he takes the role of a dictator. Perhaps a more common problem is a pastor who fails to influence the decisions of the church at all. He simply goes in the direction people want to go, which is not leadership; thus, he is not equipping the people in his church to do good work. Neither of these leadership styles will be effective in equipping those under the pastor's leadership to do good work.

Knowing your place on the leadership spectrum doesn't mean you are unable to lead; it just means you know the position and ways in which you must lead. As the provost of NOBTS, I (Norris) have responsibility to lead the faculty, but many of the faculty lead up in a variety of ways. One faculty member suggested an organization we might join with benefits for our faculty and school. I wasn't aware of the organization and likely wouldn't have known about it without the faculty member's help. Last year, our faculty received thousands of dollars in benefits all because a faculty member took the time to investigate a good opportunity and bring it to my attention. Clearly, he was leading up.

As you consider the areas where you have influence as a student, you must identify and lead within the role that you have been given. If you volunteer to serve in the nursery at a local church, then you need to realize that you are to submit to the policies and procedures the church has in place for volunteers. By working within the boundaries of the organization, you become a model for those working with you to do better work. If you find significant issues with the policies and procedures, discuss these with your supervisor and equip that person to do better work in the leadership role. What you must avoid is doing your own thing. Working outside the boundaries set for your role will result in poor performance and an inability to help others do the work they are charged with doing.

Identifying your role on the leadership spectrum requires intentionally thinking through the appropriate ways in which you can have influence. Taking the following steps will aid you as you seek your role in leadership:

1. *Do the good work that you are given to do.* Both of us serve in leadership roles in our organizations. If students at our schools were to ask us how to get involved in leadership, our answer would depend on whether they are doing good work themselves. If you do good work, then you are ready to equip others to do good work. If you do not do good work, then you will likely have a negative effect on the work of others.

2. *Know the mission of your organization.* For work to be good, it must flow from the mission of an organization. Athletic teams are deemed good or bad based on how well they accomplish their mission—to win. Likewise, individual athletes are assessed based on their contribution to the mission of the team. If you don't know the mission of a group of people, then you cannot be an effective leader. If you want to be a leader in the classroom, read the syllabus. If you desire to be a leader in a fraternity, know the purpose for the group and the story behind why it exists.

3. *Ask those in leadership over you to help you learn how to equip others.* Good leaders want to draw others into the task of leadership. That means that many of the people who are in leadership over you want to help you learn how to work alongside them in equipping others to do good work. Ask those in leadership over you not only how you can help, but how you need to interact within the group of people with whom you work. If you are curious about the boundaries of your authority or influence, ask those in leadership over you to help you define these perimeters.

4. *Make sure leadership is about service and not status.* Healthy leadership roles are about equipping others to do good work, not about climbing a ladder of influence so that you end up at the top of your organization. This does not mean

that it is wrong to want to have greater influence over the groups with which you work. Your desire, however, must be to have influence for the sake of equipping others to do good work.

Put Yourself under Godly Leaders

One of the most valuable ways I (Cory) learned to be a leader was by working as a camp counselor in Alabama when I was in high school and college. Working as a camp counselor is a clinic in leadership no matter where you work later because it puts you in a position of direct leadership over the campers. My experience at the camp was even more valuable because I was blessed to work for one of the godliest leaders I have ever met. My boss when working for the camp was a guy named Steve Stephens. The key to Steve's leadership style was that it was always focused on the campers. One of the ways Steve made sure we stayed focused on the campers was the way we ate at mealtimes. Counselors were to eat with their campers, not with one another; we couldn't waste the opportunity to minister to the students in our group. Campers were to go through the serving line first and then, when we knew the campers had gotten plenty to eat, the counselors could eat. Only after all the campers, counselors, and guests had been through the line did Steve fix a plate from whatever was left over. Steve's rigid mealtime policy illustrated his passion for servant leadership.

I learned something from working under Steve's leadership that I never would have learned from a book or lecture. I saw what it looks like to lead. If you are to be a kingdom leader, then you need to *see* what godly leadership looks like. As a student, you have some unique opportunities to place yourself under godly leadership. Doing so will not only allow you to participate in excellent work yourself, but it also provides you with an example for how to be a godly leader. Below are some ways you can seek out godly leaders to work with and learn from:

1. *Join a local church and form a relationship with the church leaders.* Forming a strong relationship with your pastor and other church leaders should provide you with a model of godly leadership that you can apply in multiple leadership contexts.
2. *Join Christian organizations on your campus.* Most colleges and graduate programs have Christian organizations that meet on campus. These groups are often sponsored by denominations or national Christian groups such as Baptist Collegiate Ministries, Fellowship of Christian Athletes, or Cru. One of the key features of these groups is that they provide students with mentors who include both fellow students and faculty or community sponsors. The leaders in these organizations have a vested interest in teaching you how to lead others on your campus and in your community.
3. *Seek out godly leaders in your course of study.* For some students, this may be a simple task—particularly if you are enrolled in a seminary or a Christian college. For others, however, you may need to search carefully to find strong Christian leaders in your field. If you are not aware of any Christians who teach in your field of study at your school, seek out Christians in that field in either the community where you live or online. Both of us have been influenced by leaders with whom we interact primarily through social media or email. The benefit of learning from leaders in your field of study is that they will help model for you how the material you are learning in class can equip you to help others to do good work.

Our hope is that this chapter has helped you think about leadership in a new way. Remember that the goal of kingdom leadership is not elevation of status within an organization. Instead, leadership is an act of service toward others. We pray that you use your time in education to hone your leadership skills so that you will be able to equip others to do good work for the glory of God.

8

Kingdom Relationships

James is a Christian pursuing a degree in education. He is a model student, a highly productive person, and an effective leader in several organizations both on and off campus. He teaches a youth Sunday school class in a local church. Most people really like James and recognize his success in many areas of life. James seems like a model kingdom student. Despite his success in these areas, James is not happy.

If you pull back the curtain on James's life, you will find that he is struggling in his relationships. He has focused so much on his work at college that he rarely calls home. He has friends on campus, but he rarely sees them outside of working in the organizations he leads. He loves the church where he serves, but he does not feel close to anyone there. Despite his success in life, James feels lonely.

In addition to this feeling of loneliness, James has several emotional and spiritual struggles. He has a younger brother who has begun to struggle with drug addiction, and he wants to help but does not know how. James thought he was going to marry the girl he dated throughout his freshman year. Then they broke up, and she is now dating one of James's friends. James has been responsible in the way he has treated her, but he is hurt by what has become of their relationship. As James focuses on being a good student and leader, he is letting his personal health slide. He had to spend the money his parents sent him for his birthday to buy some new clothes because most of his were becoming uncomfortably tight.

James's spiritual health is following a similar trajectory to his emotional and physical health. He wants to feel close to God and is pursuing his work and degree in order to be obedient to God, but he rarely spends time with God in prayer. He struggles to read the Bible on a regular basis and does not always feel closer to God when he does. James is trying to live as a faithful member of Jesus's kingdom, but he doesn't feel like life in Jesus's kingdom is a very happy one. The problem that James is facing is that his success as a student and leader has come at the expense of his relationships—relationships with his family, his friends, and with the God who made him and loves him.

James is a fictional character; we made him up to serve as an illustration. The truth, however, is that we have known dozens of students like James and have each lived out a bit of James's story ourselves. One of the reasons that stories like this are so commonly lived out among students is that it is easy to focus on being successful at the expense of other people. Productivity, leadership, and academic skills are not necessarily bad for relationships. The problem for students is that they sometimes focus on these areas at the expense of the people in their lives.

Kingdom students must prioritize relationships during their time in college. On the one hand, this is out of necessity to be the sort of student you ought to be. Healthy interactions with other people will equip you to be a productive thinker and leader throughout your studies. On the other hand, prioritizing relationships is about far more than just succeeding at your studies. Your time as a student offers you an opportunity to form deep friendships with others and to deepen your ability to form and live in healthy relationships throughout your life. In order to have increasingly healthy connections, we need to focus on some truths about why relationships matter to kingdom students.

God Creates and Re-creates Us as Relational Beings

Many people tell themselves that their work is too important for them to focus on relationships, too. Such thinking destroys friendships, marriages, childhoods, and souls. The belief that relationships can be sacrificed on the altar of work is a direct contradiction to the message of the Bible. The Scriptures provide a powerful antidote to such poisonous thinking by telling us of God's design for humanity. The sequence of Genesis 2 is important: God creates the man, places him in the garden of Eden, gives him good work to do (to guard the garden and work in it), and gives him a rule to follow to live in obedience (Gen 2:7–17). After all these things have been done, God himself looks at the man he has made, says, "It is not good for the man to be alone," and then creates the woman to be in fellowship with the man (Gen 2:18). In other words, God shows us in creation that good work in a good place is not enough. We are made to need others. We are made for relationships. Richard Plass and James Cofield argue that our very souls are relational. They remind us that "at the core of our being is this truth—we are designed for and defined by our relationships."[1]

The entire Bible makes it clear that we are created for relationships. When God created humankind, he put us not only in relationship with one another, but also with himself. If we are to be faithful subjects in Jesus's kingdom, we need to take God's emphasis on relationships very seriously. In order to enjoy and grow in our relationships, we need to be conscious of how God has designed us to relate to ourselves, to others, and to him.

---

[1] Richard Plass and James Cofield, *The Relational Soul: Moving from False Self to Deep Connection* (Downers Grove, IL: InterVarsity Press, 2014), 12.

When we think of the people to whom we relate, we rarely think of ourselves. The way we think of ourselves, however, affects the way we relate to others and to God. The Bible makes plain to us that God is three persons—the Father, the Son, and the Holy Spirit. God is, therefore, a personal God. God also makes us to be personal people. This means that we exist as individuals, not just as part of a collective. You are not "one with nature"; you are a separate individual who exists, thinks, and feels as a person in the world in which God has placed you. God's good design for us is to be obedient to him as we make choices as individuals. We see in Genesis that God created humanity and then gave them a good command to obey:

> "You are free to eat from any tree of the garden, but you must not eat from the tree of the knowledge of good and evil, for on the day you eat from it, you will certainly die." (2:16–17)

God's design for us is to obey his commands and in doing so continually enjoy our relationship with him. We all know this is not how things work out, not for Adam and Eve, not for you and me.

As individuals, we make bad choices. Adam and Eve failed to keep God's command and instead used the individuality God gave them to look for something good outside of what God provided. God created Adam and Eve with the ability to make choices that affected their relationship to other people and to God. They made a choice that was destructive to all their relationships. All of us follow in their footsteps. We all make decisions seeking to find goodness outside of what God has made good, and all our relationships are damaged in the process.

We are often tempted to fix our relationships by trying harder and making better decisions. This is not a bad impulse, and we do need to try harder to choose what is good. If we are honest with ourselves, however, then we should all admit that trying harder is not enough. The apostle Paul understood that just making up his mind to do the right thing would not work. That is why he wrote in Rom 7:15–17,

For I do not understand what I am doing, because I do not practice what I want to do, but I do what I hate. Now if I do what I do not want to do, I agree with the law that it is good. So now I am no longer the one doing it, but it is sin living in me.

If we are to have healthy relationships, we must first understand that something is foundationally wrong with us at an individual level. When we consider the conflicts we have with other people, we need to understand that we too are part of the problem. God created us to enjoy healthy and whole relationships. However, all our relationships are flawed because they involve imperfect people.

Not only does sin corrupt our behavior, but it also corrupts the behavior of others. God designed interpersonal relationships for our good, but because we now live in a world corrupted by sin, not all relationships are positive. In fact, the relationships that were designed for our greatest good are the ones that become the most destructive when things go wrong. For instance, God, in his goodness to us, designed the family to love and raise children. Unfortunately, sin corrupts even family relationships, and some of the deepest emotional pain we feel is due to damaging relationships with parents, siblings, spouses, or children. In addition to these, we also find ourselves hurt by relationships with friends, classmates, professors, and coworkers.

Because of the brokenness of relationships, many people try to minimize the impact of relationships with others in their lives. Consider the story at the beginning of this chapter. Our hypothetical student James was having trouble because of the way people like his brother and ex-girlfriend behaved. People in similar circumstances are often tempted to keep their heads down and ignore others. "You do you," we might say; after all, you can't control the behavior of others. But remember, you were *created* for relationships. Ignoring the influence others have on you will not work. Plass and Cofield observe that "we are designed by God to be influenced by others."[2] God made you to need relationships. You may need to distance yourself from some people (more on that later), but you cannot cut yourself off from relating to others. Your goal must be establishing and cultivating healthy relationships, not withdrawing from them altogether.

What hope do sinners like all of us have to live in healthy relationships with one another? We have already seen that sin destroys our abilities to consistently make right relational decisions and the abilities of others to do the same. Many of us feel this in a strong way. We have been deeply hurt by others, perhaps to the point of abuse. The pain we feel joins with the frustration of not being able to get our relationships right even when we want to do so. What solution is left for us as emotionally and spiritually broken people?

Only God is free from the destructive power of sin. Our sin destroys our relationships with one another and with God. God, however, is without sin. He alone is capable of healthy relationships. The good news is that he offers to restore our ability to live in healthy relationships through the work of Jesus Christ. We were created for healthy relationships, which we destroyed through our sin. So God, in his extraordinary goodness to us, offers to restore us to the good relationships he intended through re-creating us in Jesus Christ. Paul confessed that he had no hope of doing the right things because of the sin that corrupted him, but his message was one of hope because he also observed, "if anyone is in Christ, he is a new creation; the old has passed away, and see, the new has come" (2 Cor 5:17). Not only were we created for relationships, we were also re-created for relationships.

Often, we are afraid of the idea of becoming "new creations." We might say that we like ourselves just the way we are. Society is quick to tell us that we need to "be true to ourselves" and to "live out our truth." The problem is that we humans are born broken and what we think is truth is often a lie. C. S. Lewis said that

---

[2] Plass and Cofield, *Relational Soul*, 47.

becoming new creatures "means losing what we now call 'ourselves.' Out of our selves into Christ we must go."[3] When we are in Christ, we find that our relationships are restored not only with others, but also with ourselves. The new creation Christ works in us is the only way for us to have healthy relationships with others; it is also the only way to be the people we are supposed to be. Lewis continued his thoughts about the new creation by saying, "The more we get what we now call 'ourselves' out of the way and let Him take us over, the more truly ourselves we become."[4]

As we continue to discuss relationships, we share some practical advice that will help you develop and maintain better relationships as a student and throughout your life. The advice we offer is based on biblical truth but will be helpful for Christians and non-Christians alike. We do invite you, however, to consider the biblical message that our relationships are broken and can be truly restored only through Jesus. People of all faiths can learn to be wise in their relationships and mask the brokenness, but only Jesus offers the re-creation that is necessary to restore your relationship with God.

Healthy Relationships Lay a Foundation for Good Work

Because relationships are a part of the creative order, we should not be surprised to find that healthy relationships are foundational to good work. In our discussion of leadership, we established that all vocations require working with other people. In other words, you will never have a job in which you do not interact with others in some capacity. If your work is to be productive, then you need to be wise in the way you interact with the people in your work environment.

Healthy relationships are also vital to your success as a student. Education takes place within a community. The education that you receive as you pursue your degree will take place not only

---

[3] C. S. Lewis, *Mere Christianity* (New York: HarperCollins, 2001), 224.

[4] Lewis, 225.

in classrooms and libraries, but also in coffee shops, dorm rooms, and community spaces around your campus. One of the great values of higher education is that it places you in a community. To be successful—academically, spiritually, and psychologically—as a student, you must learn to form and maintain healthy relationships with those in your community.

I (Cory) believe that one of the greatest things I learned during my college and graduate school career was how to relate well with others. I remember coming back to my dorm room after my first day of classes. My roommate, whom I had just met the week before, was sitting on his bed watching TV. I realized that he and I were stuck together for an entire year. We were very different people. He was an exceptionally neat person—especially for an eighteen-year-old—and I was . . . not. I liked to have friends over to our room late into the night, talking about sports or theology; he liked to turn the lights out and go to sleep by 10:30. As different as we were, the fact that we were stuck together meant that we had to learn to communicate with each other and treat each other with respect. It was a good year. We both had different living arrangements the next academic year, but we continued to respect each other. I look back on that situation with grateful appreciation for the opportunity to learn to live in community with someone who is different from me.

Higher education also places you in community with people from diverse backgrounds. You may have grown up without interacting with people from other cultures. If you did interact with people from other cultures, it was likely in school; but you left school and came home at the end of the day and immersed yourself in your family life. Each comes from a particular cultural background, and there is nothing wrong with the fact that for the vast majority of us, we first learn how to form relationships with people from our own culture. The Bible, however, makes it clear that Jesus brings all types of people into his kingdom. In the book of Revelation, John sees a vision of people before the throne of God, and he notes that "there was a vast multitude from every nation, tribe, people, and language, which no one could number, standing before the throne and before the Lamb" (Rev 7:9b). Your time in higher education places you in community with people from multiple cultures. For kingdom students, this provides an opportunity to acclimate to life in the multicultural kingdom of Jesus!

Kingdom students should care about healthy relationships because God has designed us to flourish in the context of relationships. But because we are all flawed sinners, healthy relationships do not come naturally to us. We need to be aware of this fact and cultivate skills that allow us to increase our ability to live in healthy relationships with God, with others, and with ourselves.

9

A Strategy for Kingdom Relationships

When we say that this chapter lays out a strategy for kingdom relationships, we do not mean that relationships themselves can be reduced to strategies. Relationships are not mathematic formulas; you cannot ensure healthy relationships simply by following a step-by-step method. Developing and maintaining healthy relationships does, however, require intentionality. Our goal in this chapter is to give you some practical advice on how to be intentional in relating to others as a kingdom student.

Healthy relationships are extremely rewarding. We have already established that humanity was created for communion with one another and with God. We remind you of this so that you will know how vital this section should be for you as a student and as a person. Even though relationships are important, it is easy for students to place them on the back burner. The other areas we discuss in this book are skills that are required of most college students. Your studies will force you to hone your skills in academics, productivity, and leadership. Out of all the skills we cover in this book, developing healthy relationships may have the least impact on your GPA. But remember, GPA is not the main concern for kingdom students. These students seek a far higher goal in their education—to foster their ability to glorify God through kingdom service. Being able to relate well to others is vital for growing as servants in Jesus's kingdom.

Participate in Healthy Community

The Christian faith provides a particular understanding of community. Christians understand that being a part of the church includes coming together. The Bible emphasizes the communal identity of the people of God. God creates people to be together, as we have already seen in Genesis 2. God calls out the entire family of Abraham to become a special nation of people in Genesis 12. Jesus promises that he is especially present whenever believers come together in his name (Matt 18:20). Christian unity is a major theme of Paul's writings as he consistently calls believers to work, live, and worship together (see Rom 12:3–8; Phil 1:27–30; and Col 3:13 just to name a few). For Christians, participating in community is done in obedience to the story and commands of Scripture.

As a student, you have dozens of opportunities to get involved in campus life. Campuses are filled with fraternities, sororities, intramurals, ministry groups, and special interest organizations. In addition, opportunities to build personal relationships abound while you are in college. You will probably never again be as surrounded by people your age with the time to invest in friendships as you are during your time pursuing a degree. However, the new opportunities for community that you encounter as a student do not replace all your old community environments. Your family and friends from outside of campus life should continue to be some of the richest groups in which you experience healthy community— even if only virtually at times. In addition to campus and family life, you also can participate in the community of a local church. These various opportunities for community give you many options for forming healthy relationships during your studies.

Despite all of these options for community, many students feel a sense of loneliness during their time in school. If you are feeling as if you are surrounded by groups of people but do not fit in with any of them, know that you are not alone. Many students feel this way. Both of us, in fact, have known many students who felt that fitting in was one of their main struggles. You may be tempted to believe that the feeling of loneliness is something you have to endure throughout your studies. After all, education is a transitional period of life, so maybe you can just put up with the loneliness until graduation.

But if God has called you to pursue an academic degree, then he will equip you to be in community with others while you are in this season of your life. Community takes time to develop, so know that these friendships may take time to form. There are some intentional things you can do to pursue healthy community as a student. If, however, you are suffering from depression that prevents you from having healthy relationships, we encourage you to seek help. Most educational institutions have someone you can talk to confidentially about these issues. If you don't know whom to speak with, begin with the dean of students, who can direct you to resources that can help.

Before you can participate in healthy community, you need to identify which communities are healthy. God created us to live in community with one another. For community relationships to be healthy, they need to involve groups that allow us to be honest about who we are and encourage us to grow into the people God has created us to be. The best environment for this type of community is a local church. We encourage you to find a church in or near the place where you live that offers you a chance to be in community with believers who are striving to live their lives in obedience to God. We want to encourage you to do more than just attend worship at a local church. Find a small group to participate in and be willing to involve yourself in community.

Campus organizations also offer you an opportunity to participate in community with other students. Christian campus groups such as Baptist Collegiate Ministries (BCM), Cru (formerly Campus Crusade), Reformed University Fellowship (RUF), Fellowship of Christian Athletes (FCA), and InterVarsity Christian Fellowship are all great places to seek out such community.

In addition to joining campus organizations, being selective about your friends is important. If you spend your time around people who participate in destructive behavior, you will likely begin doing so yourself. Surrounding yourself with friends who love you as you are and encourage you to grow into the person God has created you to be is an essential element of healthy community.

Once you have identified healthy communities in which you can get involved, you need to participate in some of those groups. Getting involved is the first step toward healthy community because healthy community grows only through experience. Plass and Cofield argue that community can help us foster healthy relationships, but can do so only if we participate in it. They observe, "We cannot recalibrate our relational capacity by reading books . . . or discussing ideas. An attachment pattern that nurtures trust requires actual and personal relationships."[1] In other words, in order to benefit from a healthy community, you need to dive headfirst into a healthy community. Make friends, show up for campus events, and get involved in a church. Such practices are foundational to living in healthy community.

Set Appropriate Boundaries in Your Relationships

One of the most significant challenges to developing and maintaining healthy relationships is the fact that you are never in full control of your interactions with other people. No human relationship is naturally healthy, because we are all fallen people; thus, every human relationship involves multiple broken and sinful people.

---

[1] Richard Plass and James Cofield, *The Relational Soul: Moving from False Self to Deep Connection* (Downers Grove, IL: InterVarsity Press, 2014), 115.

Though it is difficult, we are able to change many of the negative ways our behavior affects our relationships. What we cannot control is how the behavior of others affects our relationships. That's why, in order to be an emotionally healthy individual, you need to set boundaries to distinguish between what you can control in relationships and what you cannot.

The Importance of Boundaries

Henry Cloud and John Townsend argue that "Boundaries define us. They define *what is me* and *what is not me*."[2] If we are to have healthy interactions with others, then we must recognize that there are boundaries to our roles in those relationships. There are things for which we are responsible (that which is me) and things for which other people are responsible (that which is not me).

Understanding boundaries equips you to take appropriate responsibility in your relationships. This is especially important during times of transition in your life, such as college, when you are learning new roles of responsibility. For many students, the transition from adolescence to adulthood creates issues of relationship boundaries with their parents.

Adults have different boundaries with their parents than do children and teenagers. As a child, you need your parents' help for almost everything, so all the responsibility in the relationship is on your parents. As you grow into adulthood, the boundaries of your responsibility broaden. You must take increased responsibility for yourself. You cannot have a healthy adult relationship with your parents if you continue to see them as having all the responsibility for areas of your life such as your finances, career, and education.

Recognizing our boundaries also allows us to see which elements in our relationship are not under our control. We may think

---

[2] Henry Cloud and John Townsend, *Boundaries: When to Say Yes, How to Say No to Take Control of Your Life* (Grand Rapids: Zondervan, 2017), 31.

that taking all the responsibility in a relationship is an act of service. After all, as members of Jesus's kingdom, don't we want to serve others and "carry one another's burdens" (Gal 6:2)? We certainly need to be willing to serve others, but the Bible makes it clear that we are not in control of other people's actions and feelings. If we are to have healthy interactions with others, we need to know when it is time to accept that we are not in control of what they do.

Accepting that you are not in control of other people's actions sounds easy, but it is not. Again, thinking of how this concept impacts your relationship with your parents is helpful. Not only do students have to adjust to the changing boundary between child and parent, parents have to do so as well. Often college students find that their parents struggle with the new boundaries in their relationship. Parents who struggle with their children's changing roles in life may expect them to take new responsibility for finances and daily routine, yet still desire to have the same authority over how students spend their own money and time as when those children were young. My (Norris's) oldest daughter just began her college career. Please believe us when we tell you that relinquishing control is not easy for parents to do, so be patient with them!

Relationships with parents are not the only ones where respecting boundaries is difficult. Students often experience struggles with boundaries in their relationships with professors, friends, and romantic partner. Being aware of the need for boundaries in all your relationships enables you to work toward healthy relationships.

Relating to God, Others, and Self

My (Cory's) most miserable experiences as a student involved failures in relationships. As a college student I experienced the heartbreak of feeling like I was in love with a girl who knew for sure she was not in love with me. Another painful experience was leaving home after a weekend visit to return to college knowing that my parents and I were angry at each other. For nearly my entire academic career, I struggled to maintain healthy sleep and eating habits, often going long periods of time fueled by too little sleep and too many cheeseburgers. My relationship with God was also a major area of concern during seasons of my life as a student. I would go through periods when I didn't make any time for communing with God through prayer, Bible reading, and worship. Other times I prayed, read my Bible, and worshiped with other believers, yet still felt far away from God.

God has been good to me, and, while I still struggle to maintain healthy relationships, today I have a happy marriage, a great relationship with my parents, a healthier lifestyle, and greater consistency experiencing God's presence in my devotional life. As I remember these struggles, however, I realize they caused me far more pain and anxiety throughout my time as a student than did any professor, research assignment, or class. The struggles I experienced can be broken into three areas—relationship with God, relationship with others, and relationship with self. One of the best ways for us to have healthy relationships is to consider how God's design for our relationships affects each of these areas:

1. *Our relationship with God is foundational to all other relationships.* When Jesus was asked which commandment in the law (which tells us how God wants us to relate to him and to one another) was the greatest, he said, "Love the Lord your God with all your heart, with all your soul, and with all your mind. This is the greatest and most important command" (Matt 22:37–38). Our relationship with God is the most important because it is foundational to all of the other relationships in our lives. This doesn't mean that only Christians can have good relationships with others. Christians, however, cannot have a loving relationship with God without that relationship radiating out into their love for others.

2. *God commands us to love others.* Jesus not only told us the most important commandment, but he also went on to say, "The second is like it: Love your neighbor as yourself" (Matt 22:39). If we are obedient to God's command to

love him, we must also be obedient to his command to love others. By viewing our relationships with others in this way, we come to see healthy interactions with people as a product of our healthy relationship with God. This means that we take our responsibilities in relationships seriously because God desires our relationship with him to affect our interactions with others. It also gives us a reason for respecting the boundaries in other people's lives. Because we realize that only God loves us perfectly, we know that our love for others is an extension of his love but is not the greatest love they will experience.

3. *God commands us to have a healthy relationship with ourselves.* As we consider Jesus's command "love your neighbor as yourself," we must realize that to have a healthy relationship with others, we must also have a healthy relationship with self. God created us to flourish. The Bible makes it clear that the life Jesus offers to us is a fulfilling life. In John 10:10 the life Jesus offers to those in his kingdom is contrasted with the destructive life found outside of Jesus. Jesus reminds his disciples, "A thief comes only to steal and kill and destroy. I have come so that they may have life and have it in abundance." This does not mean that people in the kingdom of Jesus are to expect to get whatever we want out of life. It means something far better; those who live in the kingdom are meant to live fulfilling lives as they serve King Jesus and enjoy his presence!

Our final advice to you is that you take relationships seriously. Of all the skills we cover in this book, relationships are the most difficult to break into a simple how-to list. If anything, this speaks to the importance of relationships in your life as a student. Maintaining healthy ones will help you in every area of your life and will equip you for service in Jesus's kingdom both during your time in school and for the rest of your days.

CONCLUSION

Remember that being a kingdom student begins with a unique approach to education. Kingdom students view their education as contributing to the work God is calling them to do as a part of Jesus's kingdom. One day you will graduate and no longer have to attend class or turn in homework assignments. Your service to the kingdom of Jesus, however, is a lifelong endeavor. College and graduate school offer exceptional opportunities to serve Jesus's kingdom. Such opportunities will only increase throughout the rest of your life. As God allows you to learn new things and hone new skills, he will also present you with new opportunities to use what you learn for the service of Jesus's kingdom.

Many students will graduate and will never again think of themselves as academics. Ceasing to be an academic does not mean that you will not still have opportunities to put your academic skills to work. In the workplace, in your family, in churches, and in other areas of life, you will have chances to put your old skills of reading and studying into play in order to serve others and accomplish the work that is set before you.

Whatever you do after graduation, you will be able to use what you have learned in this season of life to be more productive in future endeavors. Your ability to be productive during your time as a student gives you an opportunity to be productive through the rest of your life. Remember that the goal of productivity is not to increase the number of tasks you can do, but to multiply the amount of good work you can accomplish. Simply put, do not forget that the greatest value of being productive is that it increases your service to others.

As you move toward graduation, consider that you are entering into a world that is in desperate need of leaders. On the one hand, leaders are needed in national and global arenas. Perhaps God will use what you have learned about equipping others to do good work to fill the need for leadership at these levels. Leaders are needed not only on a large scale, however, but also at the local level. Whether or not you are called upon to be a politician or CEO, you will need to lead in your community, church, and family.

Perhaps the area of student life that will have the most significant impact on your life after academic work is that of relationships. The friends you make during your studies often become lifelong friends who continue to enrich your life long after graduation. What you learn about relationships—good ones and bad ones—will likewise affect your ability to glorify God through your future relationships.

In this conclusion, we have said much about your life beyond school, but we realize you are possibly several years away from finishing your studies. We point you toward how the concepts covered in this book affect life beyond school because we want you to consider the importance of growing in these areas during your time as a student. Remember, you are not in your degree program by mistake. God, who moves all things for his glory and the good of those who love him, put you here with and for a purpose. He has called you to this time in your life to make you a better servant of the kingdom of Jesus. We pray that you make much of the opportunity he has given you.

SCRIPTURE INDEX